Diana Keuilian

THE RECIPE
Hacker

Front Table Books ❁ Cedar Fort Publishing ❁ Springville, Utah

ISBN: 978-1-4621-1539-6

Published by Front Table Books, an imprint of Cedar Fort, Inc.
2373 W. 700 S., Springville, UT, 84663
Distributed by Cedar Fort, Inc., www.cedarfort.com

LIBRARY OF CONGRESS CATALOGING-IN-PUBLICATION DATA

Keuilian, Diana, 1981-
The recipe hacker : guilt-free clean eating / Diana Keuilian.
    pages cm
Includes bibliographical references and index.
Cooking.
ISBN 978-1-4621-1539-6 (alk. paper)
1. Comfort food. 2. Health. I. Title.

TX714.K49 2014
641.5--dc23
                         2014026855

Cover and page design by Bekah Claussen
Cover design © 2014 by Lyle Mortimer
Edited by Kristen Soelberg and Rachel Munk

Cover photo by Cesar A Henriquez with creative collaboration by Rob Jaeger
Dedication photo by Brian Hamilton
Author photo by Corey Sandler

Printed in the United States of America

10 9 8 7 6 5 4 3

DEDICATION

This cookbook has truly been a labor of love. I agonized over each picture, recipe, and anecdote. My goal was to provide you with 100 wholesome recipes that your family will learn to love and choose over traditional processed foods. And if I can make you smile and inspire you to eat healthier along the way, then I'm happy.

Photo by Brian Hamilton

None of this would have been possible without the love and unending support of my husband, Bedros, and my two enthusiastic (and brutally honest) taste-testers, Andrew and Chloe. I love you guys so, so much.

This book also wouldn't have been possible without the amazing support of my blog readers and Facebook fans. You truly inspire me. Thank you so much for being on this wild ride with me.

I really don't want to start rambling here, but I simply have to mention a few more of my peeps. Cara: thank you for always dropping by at a moment's notice to taste test new recipes. And for just being awesome in general. Kristen: how many trips to the grocery store did you do for the creation of this book? Probably too many to count! Thank you for all you do! Pete: Your artistic design for RealHealthyRecipes.com makes me happy every day when I look at it! And your encouraging words mean the world.

Hope you enjoy this book! Reach out to me at RealHealthyRecipes.com and Facebook.com/RealHealthyRecipes and I'll send many more healthy recipes your way.

P.S. If I can finish this book, then you too can accomplish your big thing. I truly believe that. Let me tell you, there were moments when I thought that I'd never finish or felt I was going insane in my kitchen, piled under dirty dishes. But in the end, here we are and I'm still alive. So go on, get going on your passion project!

CONTENTS

CONTENTS

Welcome to the Recipe Hacker   vi

WELCOME TO *THE RECIPE HACKER*

My name is Diana Keuilian and I'm a recipe hacker.

One day, while putting the finishing touches on dinner, I was trying to explain to my husband, B, how much I enjoy taking an existing, traditional recipe and turning it into something healthier. I rambled on about the challenge of taking out the gluten, sugar, dairy, soy, and grains without sacrificing flavor or consistency, and what a thrill I get when my healthier version of a classic turns out to be tastier than the original.

B looked up and said, "You know what you are? You're a recipe hacker."

I wasn't sure how to take that. It sounded rather outlawish.

Then again, in a sense, I broke the recipe code when I discovered how to use wholesome ingredient substitutions to transform traditional dishes into real food masterpieces.

I love food, to a fault. Sometimes I've looked at this as a curse, like when trying to lose the baby weight, but most of the time I see it for what it is: a blessing.

Food is a blessing, and really good, flavorful food is one of the highest pleasures of this life. Going to a gourmet restaurant and having the chef's tasting menu, or taking a warm cookie out of the oven and wiping melted chocolate off your face—does it get better than this?

Food is exciting and food is fun.

But eating lots of rich foods filled with grains, gluten, dairy, cane sugar, and soy left me overly full, bloated, and prone to weight gain.

So I started hacking recipes by swapping out the heavy stuff for lighter, real food ingredients. The resulting recipe has the taste, look, and feel of the original—without the ensuing food coma!

I love food *way* too much to give up flavorful and delicious dinners, snacks, and desserts. In this cookbook I'll share with you 100 of my favorite comfort food recipes, all made without grains, gluten, dairy, cane sugar, or soy. Some of these recipes are fan favorites from my blog, RealHealthyRecipes.com, while many more are brand new creations.

I hope that you enjoy these hacked recipes as much as I enjoyed making them!

WHY HEALTHY?

You may wonder if it's worth the trouble to make healthy food, especially when fast food is so quick and convenient.

The fact is that our kids are becoming obese at a much younger age than any generation before them. Childhood obesity opens the door for a life riddled with health complications that can ultimately end in heart disease, stroke, kidney failure, amputations, blindness, or death at an early age.

My son, Andrew, was born in 2005, the same year that it was announced that our kids now have a shorter life expectancy than we do. What a wake-up call that was for me as a young new mother.

I couldn't allow my son to become a statistic.

This is where I find my motivation to take the extra time and effort to create and serve healthy food for my family.

You may feel the same way, or perhaps you've been pushed into the world of gluten-free due to allergies.

Whatever brought you to this place of wanting to cook healthy dishes, I'm so glad that you've arrived! The health and well-being of your family will be elevated and your taste buds will be rewarded.

And I'm pretty sure we will have some fun along the way too!

REAL HEALTHY INGREDIENTS

Eliminating grains, gluten, dairy, cane sugar, and soy from your kitchen certainly opens up a few gaps. Here's how I fill them with healthier ingredients.

Organic Ingredients: Whenever possible, I purchase organic ingredients. This goes for produce, meat, eggs, and pantry items. While I don't specify organic in each recipe, know that organic is preferred and will taste better and offer more nutrients.

Flax Meal: This nutritional ground seed is used to replace flour in baking.

Coconut Flour: Ground from coconut meal, this is another wonderful flour substitute.

Blanched Almond Flour: Made from ground, blanched almonds. It's one of my favorite flour substitutes.

Almond Meal: Made from ground almonds with the skins still on, almond meal is a bit heartier than blanched almond flour.

Almond Substitutes: For those of you who are unable to use almonds due to allergies, I have 2 substitutes for your baking. Grind raw sunflower seeds or gluten-free oats into a flour, and use these in a 1:1 ratio for both blanched almond flour and almond meal.

Coconut Palm Sugar: Made from dried coconut sap, this wholesome sweetener is a healthier alternative to cane sugar.

Pure Maple Syrup: Believe it or not, pure maple syrup works very well in baking.

Raw Honey: This is another one of my go-to wholesome sweeteners. It contains loads of vitamins and minerals. I always measure raw honey melted.

Coconut Milk: Thank goodness for the versatile coconut! Coconut milk is all that I use to replace dairy milk in my cooking.

Coconut Oil: This wholesome oil is my go-to in baking. It is also measured melted.

Kitchen tools that I could NOT live without (in no particular order): food processor, skillet, high-speed blender, measuring cups, measuring spoons, good mixing bowls, spiral slicer, 4-cup measuring cup with spout, griddle, spatula, whisk, thick wood cutting board, baking sheet, mini muffin pan, muffin pan, brownie pan, donut pan, and good knives.

A ~~DISCLAIMER~~ ~~WARNING~~ MESSAGE BEFORE WE BEGIN

Let me introduce you to the Lazy Chef. <-- That's me.

I'm not a painstakingly precise person. If I could throw away my measuring cups, I would. I like to cook off instincts rather than instruction. But I can't exactly write a recipe without some precision.

While in the kitchen, I have this need for speed and efficiency. And so I cut as many corners as I can, without sacrificing the end result. As much as I love to cook, there's a big world out there calling to me!

So you will notice that I don't have a lot of patience for things like sifting flour. A few strokes with a fork does the job, right? Come on, I need to post a recipe on Facebook.

I like to think of this as my being really efficient and not lazy, but the jury is still out on that. If you love to sift and do any other number of extra, fancy steps that you notice I leave out, please feel free to get as fancy as you'd like. I will applaud your efforts (while I post on Facebook . . .).

All right, let's have some fun.

BREAKFASTS

. . . worth waking up for

BANANA PANCAKES

Can't you see that it's just raining? Ain't no need to go outside . . . My fellow Jack Johnson fans are grinning right now. More often than not I'm grooving to his mellow tunes while making messes in the RHR (Real Healthy Recipes) kitchen. If you aren't familiar with the catchy song "Banana Pancakes," then look it up or, better yet, put it on while you whip up a batch of these tender, delicious, grain-free pancakes. *Pretend like it's the weekend now . . .*

Quick Tip: To make your pancakes fluffier, place a glass lid over them as they cook. Don't ask me why! It's a combination of heat, baking soda, and magic. This trick takes a little more time, since you'll need to cook each pancake individually, but it really increases the fluffiness factor!

Prep: 15 minutes ✲ *Cook:* 8 minutes ✲ *Makes:* 4 servings

---

1 ripe banana, mashed

2 eggs

¼ cup coconut palm sugar

1 Tbsp. vanilla extract

¼ tsp. almond extract

1½ cups blanched almond flour

½ tsp. baking soda

½ tsp. sea salt

coconut oil for greasing the griddle

---

1) Preheat your pancake griddle or large skillet over medium-high heat.

2) Combine the banana, eggs, coconut palm sugar, vanilla extract, and almond extract in a food processor. Blend until smooth.

3) In a medium bowl, combine the almond flour, baking soda, and sea salt. (Or don't. If you need pancakes lickety-split, then skip this step and settle for a few possible lumps. I won't judge.) Add the dry ingredients to the food processor and pulse until smooth. Let the batter sit for 10–15 minutes, if you can muster the patience. This will help your pancakes bind together.

4) Use a paper towel to carefully rub coconut oil on your preheated griddle or skillet. Reduce the heat to medium. Use a ¼ cup to scoop the batter onto the griddle in nice big circles. When bubbles form, flip the pancakes to cook on the other side. Serve with fresh fruit, pure maple syrup, and your favorite tunes. Enjoy!

SWEDISH PANCAKES

Swedish pancakes were my favorite breakfast while growing up. I'd enjoy a big stack of these thinly rolled cakes on my birthday every year. The best part was a big pat of fruit-spiked butter melting on top. Mmmmmm, pass the syrup. Naturally, I hacked this favorite recipe, leaving out the grains, gluten, dairy, and cane sugar.

Quick Tip: To make your own dairy-free, fruit-spiked butter, soften some coconut butter and use an electric mixer to whip it. Add a few spoonfuls of fruit-only jam or blended fresh berries. Scoop the mixture into a small bowl, and chill in the fridge until pancake time.

Prep: 10 minutes ✿ *Cook:* 20 minutes ✿ *Makes:* 4 servings

---

4 eggs

2 cups coconut milk, full fat

½ cup blanched almond flour

¼ cup arrowroot starch

1 Tbsp. coconut palm sugar

¼ tsp. sea salt

½ tsp. vanilla extract

---

1) Preheat a pancake griddle or large skillet. Lightly grease with coconut oil.

2) Combine all of the ingredients in a food processor. Blend until smooth. The batter will be thin.

3) Pour the batter into a large measuring cup with a spout. This will help you easily pour the batter. Pour a ring of batter onto the preheated griddle and allow it to set for about 10 seconds. Slowly pour more batter into the center of the ring until filled. Cook until the bottom is lightly browned. Flip over and cook briefly until that side is browned. Serve with syrup and fresh fruit. Enjoy!

WAFFLES

Who doesn't love a lazy weekend breakfast of waffles and fresh fruit? Too bad most waffle recipes are filled with gluten and refined sugar. These grain-free waffles are the perfect weekend indulgence that won't leave you bloated and lethargic. Instead, this breakfast of champions will fill you with real food energy to power you through your active weekend. Go get 'em, Tiger!

Quick Tip: Try this simple, tropical fruit topping on your waffles. Slice a mango and banana into a bowl. Add halved segments from a tangerine. Mix in a sprinkle of ground cinnamon. Yum, an instant Hawaiian vacation! Or not. But it does taste good.

Prep: 25 minutes ✿ *Cook:* 4 minutes ✿ *Makes:* 4 servings

---

4 eggs

½ cup canned coconut milk, full fat

2 Tbsp. pure maple syrup

1 tsp. vanilla extract

1 cup blanched almond flour

1 Tbsp. coconut flour

1 tsp. baking soda

¼ tsp. sea salt

¼ tsp. ground cinnamon

---

1) Preheat a waffle iron and lightly grease with coconut oil. Combine the eggs, coconut milk, syrup, and vanilla extract in a bowl. Mix well.

2) Combine the almond flour, coconut flour, baking soda, sea salt, and cinnamon in another bowl. Add to the wet ingredients and mix well.

3) Pour the batter onto the preheated waffle iron and cook according to the manufacturer's instructions. Serve with fresh fruit and pure maple syrup. Enjoy!

CINNAMON ROLLS

When I was growing up, back when hanging out at the mall and eating gluten were both in vogue, I made many stops at the Cinnabon counter. All of those after-school cinnamon rolls probably explain how I landed the childhood nickname of Baby Fat. Kids can be cruel and brutally honest. By the time I was entering 9th grade, I had packed nearly 150 pounds onto my 5-foot frame. There was no denying the fact that I was chubby.

At the time, I had no concept of nutrition. No one pointed out that the majority of my diet was sugar and grains, which were causing me to gain weight. It took years of struggling with my weight and reading about nutrition to discover that once I cut out the sugar and the grains, my body would drop the excess fat.

Now it's been years since I've tasted a traditional cinnamon roll. When a craving hits, I make this grain- and refined sugar-free recipe for cinnamon rolls. To recreate the buttery, cinnamon goo, I used coconut oil, coconut crystals, golden raisins, chopped pecans, and ground cinnamon. (Lots of ground cinnamon!) You'll never need a traditional cinnamon roll after trying this recipe.

Quick Tip: These 3 steps are important for successfully rolling and slicing the dough:

1) Chill the dough for at least 15 minutes before rolling.

2) Use the parchment paper to assist you in rolling, don't attempt to roll just with your hands.

3) Use a string to cut the rolls, rather than a knife. This helps make a clean cut that doesn't squish the rest of the roll.

Prep: 30 minutes ❁ *Bake:* 20 minutes ❁ *Oven:* 350°F ❁ *Makes:* 15 rolls

---

2½ cups blanched almond flour

¼ cup coconut flour

¼ tsp. baking soda

½ tsp. sea salt

½ cup plus 2 Tbsp. coconut oil, divided

¼ cup plus 2 Tbsp. raw honey, divided

2 eggs

1 Tbsp. plus 2 tsp. vanilla extract, divided

¾ cup coconut palm sugar, divided

2 Tbsp. ground cinnamon

¼ cup golden raisins

¼ cup pecans

¼ tsp. almond extract

---

1) Preheat the oven to 350°F. Lightly grease a pan with coconut oil.

2) Combine the almond flour, coconut flour, baking soda, and sea salt in a medium bowl and mix to remove any lumps. Combine ¼ cup coconut oil, 2 tablespoons raw honey, eggs, 1 tablespoon vanilla extract, and ¼ cup coconut palm sugar in another medium bowl and mix well. Combine the wet and dry ingredients and mix well. Chill the dough for 15 minutes.

3) Cut two rectangular pieces of parchment paper and place the dough in between them. Use a rolling pin to flatten the dough evenly into a large rectangle. Remove the top piece of parchment paper.

4) In a small bowl, combine ½ cup coconut palm sugar, ground cinnamon, 2 tablespoons coconut oil, and the golden raisins and chopped pecans. Sprinkle this filling mixture over the flattened dough, and then carefully roll it up. Use the bottom parchment paper to assist in rolling the dough—this works better than using your hands. Use a serrated knife to carefully slice the dough into 15 rolls. Or use a string to wrap around the roll and pull tight, cutting the dough. Carefully place the pieces on your prepared pan.

5) Bake for 20 minutes.

6) In a small bowl, combine ¼ cup raw honey, ¼ cup coconut oil, ¼ teaspoon almond extract, and 2 teaspoons vanilla extract. Drizzle over the cinnamon rolls. Sprinkle with chopped pecans. Enjoy!

CINNAMON PUFFS

A big shout-out to Ree Drummond (from *The Pioneer Woman Cooks*) for this recipe. I got the idea from her French Breakfast Puffs recipe and did a little hacking. I finagled the ingredients to take out the refined sugar, butter, and white flour. Ree is shaking her head in disappointment right now. I'm sorry! It's just that those of us who don't eat refined sugar, butter, and white flour still really, really want to eat cinnamon puffy things for breakfast. She will forgive me. I hope. One day.

Quick Tip: If you're allergic to almonds, there are two wonderful substitutions you can use in a 1:1 ratio instead of almond flour: 1) Grind sunflower seeds into flour in your food processor. 2) Grind gluten-free oats into flour in your food processor. Use these substitutions in any recipe that calls for almond meal or blanched almond flour.

Prep: 20 minutes ✿ *Bake:* 25 minutes ✿ *Oven:* 350°F ✿ *Makes:* 12 muffins

2 cups blanched almond flour

⅓ cup coconut flour

1 Tbsp. baking powder

1 tsp. sea salt

½ tsp. ground nutmeg

1½ cups coconut palm sugar, divided

⅔ cup palm shortening

2 eggs

1 cup canned coconut milk, full fat

1 Tbsp. ground cinnamon

1) Preheat the oven to 350°F. Grease a 12-cup muffin tin with coconut oil.

2) Combine the blanched almond flour, coconut flour, baking powder, sea salt, and nutmeg in a medium bowl.

3) Combine 1 cup coconut palm sugar and palm shortening in a bowl and cream using an electric mixer. Add the eggs and mix well.

4) Alternately add spoonfuls of the dry ingredients and splashes of the coconut milk, beating well after each addition. The batter will be very creamy.

5) Fill the greased muffin cups with batter. Smooth the tops of each muffin. Bake for 20–25 minutes, until golden and baked through.

6) Combine the remaining ½ cup coconut palm sugar and ground cinnamon in a shallow bowl. Allow the muffins to cool, and then roll in the cinnamon sugar mixture. Serve with tea or some other hot beverage in fancy cups with delicate handles. Enjoy!

BRAN MUFFINS

My real healthy recipe-hacking philosophy on making improvements to our eating habits is simple: don't deprive. Instead simply replace unhealthy items for healthier ones. So I came up with this gluten- and refined sugar-free recipe for muffins that are just as moist and delicious as the store bought bran ones.

Quick Tip: If you don't already have a mini muffin pan, drop everything and go get one right now. It's okay, I'll wait. Seriously, mini muffin pans are a godsend when it comes to portion control. One mini muffin is all it takes to satisfy that sweet tooth.

Prep: 20 minutes ✿ *Bake:* 20 minutes ✿ *Oven:* 350°F ✿ *Makes:* 24 mini muffins

---

½ cup blanched almond flour

½ cup flax meal

1 Tbsp. coconut flour

1 tsp. baking soda

½ tsp. sea salt

½ tsp. ground cinnamon

3 eggs

half a banana

⅓ cup coconut palm sugar

2 Tbsp. pure maple syrup

¼ cup canned coconut milk, full fat

2 Tbsp. almond butter

1 tsp. vanilla extract

½ cup golden raisins

½ cup raw pecans

1 Tbsp. coconut oil

---

1) Preheat the oven to 350°F. Line a 24-cup mini muffin tin with paper liners.

2) Combine the almond flour, flax meal, coconut flour, baking soda, sea salt, and ground cinnamon in a medium bowl. Mix well.

3) Combine the eggs, banana, coconut palm sugar, maple syrup, coconut milk, almond butter, and vanilla extract in a food processor. Blend until smooth.

4) Add the dry ingredients to the food processor. Pulse until smooth. Add the raisins and pecans to the food processor. Pulse for 15 seconds. Add the melted coconut oil and pulse again until just combined.

5) Fill the mini muffin tins with batter. Bake for 15–20 minutes until golden and baked through. Cool on a wire rack for 10 minutes. Enjoy!

Keuilian

BLUEBERRY MUFFINS

Whenever I bite into a big, juicy blueberry, it brings me back to late-summer trips down to the blueberry farm.

We would drive down Farm-to-Market Road, where it would plunge down into the valley with Samish Bay sparkling off to the left, and majestic Mount Baker—tall and white—rising off to the right. The road would wind through Edison, a town so small you could hold your breath from one end to the other. Then we'd pass the Rhododendron Cafe, home to surprisingly sophisticated cuisine despite it's humble appearance and remote location. Farmhouses would whizz by, with big friendly horses and brightly colored swing sets. Finally we would pull into the blueberry farm parking lot, gravel crunching cheerfully.

The air inside the shop was sweet from the rows of blueberry flats and freshly baked blueberry pies.

On the drive home I would run my hand over the tops of the blueberry flats, fingers grabbing onto the biggest ones, teeth turning blue.

These moist blueberry muffins are low carb, protein-filled, and delicately flavored. Enjoy one for an energizing power breakfast.

Quick Tip: If you are using frozen blueberries and don't want the batter to get that greenish tint to it (ewww!), don't worry, there's a simple solution. Rinse the frozen berries in cold water several times until the runoff water becomes noticeably lighter in color. Next dry the rinsed berries with paper towels, and mix into your batter.

Prep: 20 minutes ❁ *Bake:* 25 minutes ❁ *Oven:* 350°F ❁ *Makes:* 12 muffins

---

½ coconut flour

½ tsp. sea salt

½ tsp. baking soda

6 eggs

½ cup coconut palm sugar

⅓ cup coconut oil

1 Tbsp. vanilla extract

¼ tsp. almond extract

1 cup blueberries, fresh or frozen

---

1) Preheat the oven to 350°F. Line a 12-cup muffin tin with paper liners.

2) Combine the coconut flour, sea salt, and baking soda in a small bowl. Mix well.

3) Combine the eggs, coconut palm sugar, coconut oil, vanilla extract, and almond extract in a food processor. Blend until smooth. Add the dry ingredients to the food processor. Pulse until smooth. Use a large spoon to mix in the blueberries.

4) Fill each of the muffin cups with batter. Bake for 20–25 minutes, until golden and baked through. Enjoy!

CHOCOLATE MUFFINS

I recently gave a basket of these divinely chocolate muffins to my dear friends, John and Cara Eckerman. The ensuing texts that I received were pretty accusatory. They couldn't believe that these muffins were healthy, and they asked if I used refined sugar and regular flour. Harrumph! Why is this muffin, which looks suspiciously like a cupcake, and tastes like one too, in the breakfast section instead of desserts? It's hiding vitamin-rich beets in its chocolatey depths. Totally acceptable as a nutritious breakfast, right? Nod yes. (Take that, John and Cara!)

Quick Tip: The recipe calls for canned beets (Lazy Chef, remember?) but it would also be delightful with fresh, boiled beets. To do so, place scrubbed beets in a pot of water, add a sprinkle of salt, and boil for 35–60 minutes. You'll know your beets are done when they are fork-tender.

Prep: 20 minutes ❁ *Bake:* 20 minutes ❁ *Oven:* 350°F ❁ *Makes:* 12 muffins

1 cup dark chocolate

¼ cup coconut oil

⅓ cup raw honey

2 eggs

2 tsp. vanilla extract

¼ tsp. almond extract

1 (15-oz.) can beets, drained

1 cup blanched almond flour

2 Tbsp. coconut flour

¼ cup unsweetened cocoa powder

2 tsp. baking soda

¼ tsp. sea salt

½ cup dark chocolate chips

1) Preheat the oven to 350°F. Line 12 muffin tins with paper liners.

2) Combine the dark chocolate, coconut oil, and honey in a small pot, and place in a medium skillet in an inch of water. Place over medium heat. Stir often until the chocolate mixture becomes smooth.

3) Combine the melted chocolate mixture, eggs, vanilla extract, almond extract, and beets in a food processor. Pulse until smooth.

4) In a medium bowl, combine the almond flour, coconut flour, cocoa powder, baking soda, and sea salt. Add to the wet ingredients in the food processor. Pulse until smooth. Mix the chocolate chips into the batter with a large spoon.

5) Fill each muffin tin with batter. Bake for 20 minutes, or until baked through. Serve with a sprinkle of unsweetened, shredded coconut. Share with an unsuspecting friend and harrumph when they accuse you of using refined sugar. Enjoy!

Keuilian

BREAKFAST COOKIES

Who doesn't want to eat a cookie for breakfast? I sure do. And let me tell you, it's pretty easy to get the kids to eat a cookie on their way to school. Heehee. These cookies are packed with bananas, coconut, raisins, and almonds—all very wholesome and nutrient-dense ingredients. So you can hand out breakfast cookies to the kiddos with a smile on your face, knowing that they are starting their day off right.

Quick Tip: Make a batch of these Breakfast Cookies on the weekend, and store them in an airtight container in the fridge for quick, on-the-go weekday breakfasts.

Prep: 20 minutes ❁ *Bake:* 35 minutes ❁ *Oven:* 350°F ❁ *Makes:* 20 cookies

3 ripe bananas
½ cup unsweetened apple sauce
2 Tbsp. coconut oil
1 tsp. vanilla extract
1 tsp. apple cider vinegar
⅓ cup coconut flour
1 tsp. ground cinnamon
1 tsp. baking soda
¼ tsp. sea salt
2 cups unsweetened shredded coconut
½ cup black raisins
¼ cup sliced almonds

1) Preheat the oven to 350°F. Line a baking sheet with parchment paper.

2) Combine the bananas, applesauce, coconut oil, vanilla extract, and apple cider vinegar in a food processor. Blend until smooth.

3) Combine the coconut flour, cinnamon, baking soda, and sea salt in a medium bowl.

Add the dry ingredients to the food processor. Pulse until combined. Add the shredded coconut, raisins, and sliced almonds and mix with a big spoon.

4) Place large scoops of dough, using an ice cream scooper, on the prepared baking sheet. Lightly press the balls of dough down into cookie shape. Sprinkle a few pieces of sliced almonds and raisins on each cookie. Bake for 25–35 minutes, until golden and baked through. Allow to cool for 5 minutes on the pan, and then transfer to a cooling rack. Store in an airtight container in the fridge. Enjoy!

DONUT BREAKFAST SANDWICH

Yes, this recipe is for reals. I know, it looks like something out of a fantasy, or the Paula Deen show, but it is indeed healthy. Or healthier. Let's deconstruct it. First we start with a grain-, gluten-, and refined-sugar-free baked donut. Then we dip our wholesome donut in a glaze made with coconut oil and raw honey. Next we add a nutritious egg and slices of nitrate-free bacon. Not too sinful after all . . .

Quick Tip: There are many ways to expand on this basic donut recipe, if you are so inclined. And why wouldn't you be? Here are my favorite variations:

Chocolate Glazed Donuts: Use the donut recipe below and dip in ½ cup dark chocolate melted with 1 tablespoon coconut oil. Put in the fridge for a few minutes so the chocolate hardens.

Apple Fritter Donuts: Add ½ teaspoon ground cinnamon in step 2. Add ¼ teaspoon maple extract in step 4. In a skillet, combine 1 tablespoon coconut oil, 1 small apple (finely chopped), 1 tablespoon pure maple syrup, and 1 teaspoon ground cinnamon. Cook until soft, and then fold the apple mixture into the batter in step 5.

Chocolate Donuts: Add ¼ cup unsweetened cocoa powder in step 2. Increase the maple syrup to 4 tablespoons in step 4.

Prep: 20 minutes ✺ *Bake:* 15 minutes ✺ *Oven:* 350°F ✺ *Makes:* 6 sandwiches

---

1¼ cups blanched almond flour

¼ tsp. baking soda

3 Tbsp. pure maple syrup

¼ + ¼ tsp. almond extract, divided

½ + 2 tsp. vanilla extract, divided

2 Tbsp. + ¼ cup coconut oil, divided

1 tsp. apple cider vinegar

2 eggs + 6 eggs, divided

¼ cup honey

6 bacon strips

---

1) Preheat the oven to 350°F. Grease a donut pan with coconut oil.

2) Combine the almond flour and baking soda in a small bowl.

3) Separate the egg yolks and whites. Use an electric mixer to beat the egg whites until stiff peaks form.

4) Combine the yolks, syrup, almond extract, vanilla extract, 2 tablespoons coconut oil, and vinegar in a bowl.

5) Add the dry ingredients to the wet ones. Mix to combine. Gently fold in the egg whites. Use a piping bag to pipe the batter into each of the 6 donut tins. Smooth out the tops of the donuts. Bake for 15 minutes.

6) Meanwhile, individually fry 6 eggs and cook the bacon in a skillet. Set aside.

7) Combine the honey and remaining ¼ cup coconut oil, ¼ teaspoon almond extract, and 2 teaspoons vanilla extract in a small bowl.

8) Chill the donuts for 10 minutes. Dip in the glaze and place on a tray lined with parchment paper. Chill for another 10 minutes. Slice each donut in half and fill with a fried egg and slices of bacon. Enjoy!

Keuilian

STUFFED DONUT HOLES

Donut holes are just plain awesome. Especially when they are made grain and sugar-free. But stuffed donut holes are better. Much, much better. Why? Come, do you really have to ask? Because it's stuffed with LOVE.

Quick Tip: A cake pop pan and a donut hole pan are basically the same thing. If there's a difference, then I sure haven't figured out what it is. So feel free to use either pan to make these awesome donut holes. Oh and plan to make extras, these things have a way of disappearing.

Prep: 25 minutes ✿ *Bake:* 12 minutes ✿ *Oven:* 350°F ✿ *Makes:* 20 donut holes

---

1 small apple, chopped

3 Tbsp. coconut oil, divided

4 Tbsp. raw honey, divided

1½ tsp. ground cinnamon, divided

1¼ cups blanched almond flour

¼ tsp. baking soda

¼ tsp. almond extract

½ tsp. vanilla extract

1 tsp. apple cider vinegar

2 eggs

⅓ cup coconut palm sugar

---

1) Preheat the oven to 350°F. Lightly grease a donut hole pan with coconut oil.

2) Place a skillet over medium-low heat. Add the coconut oil and chopped apple. Cook, stirring often, until soft. This takes about 5 minutes. Add the honey and cinnamon. Continue to cook for another 2 minutes. Remove from heat and allow to cool.

3) In a medium bowl, combine the almond flour, baking soda, and remaining ½ teaspoon ground cinnamon. Mix well.

4) Separate the egg yolks and whites. Use an electric mixer with a whisk attachment to whip the egg whites.

5) Combine the remaining 3 tablespoons honey, almond extract, vanilla extract, remaining 2 tablespoons coconut oil, apple cider vinegar, and yolks together in a bowl. Add the dry ingredients and mix well. Fold in the whipped egg whites. Be careful not to mix too much—we want to keep as much fluffiness as possible.

6) Fill each donut hole tin halfway with batter. Add a teaspoon of the apple mixture and cover with more batter. Bake for 8–12 minutes, until golden. Allow the donut holes to cool, and then roll in coconut palm sugar. Enjoy!

EVERYTHING BAGELS

As a former carbaholic, I take my bagels very seriously. In the order of awesomeness, there are blueberry bagels, chocolate chip bagels, jalapeño bagels, cinnamon raisin bagels, and—my all-time favorite—everything bagels. Of course, traditional bagels are such a bomb of gluten and grains that there was a time when I couldn't imagine ever enjoying one again. That prompted me to create this grain-free version of bagels, and my bagel-loving heart has been happy again ever since.

Quick Tip: Want to change up the flavor? I've got you covered. Omit the poppy seeds, sesame seeds, and dried garlic from this recipe and mix in the following after step 2 for new flavors.

Blueberry Bagels: ¼ cup coconut palm sugar, ½ cup fresh or frozen blueberries.

Chocolate Chip Bagels: ¼ cup coconut palm sugar and ½ cup mini dark chocolate chips or chopped dark chocolate.

Jalapeño Bagels: 1 tablespoon coconut palm sugar and 6 jalapeños, seeded and finely chopped.

Cinnamon Raisin Bagels: 1 tablespoon ground cinnamon, ¼ cup coconut palm sugar, and ½ cup raisins.

Prep: 20 minutes ❁ *Bake*: 25 minutes ❁ *Oven:* 350°F ❁ *Makes:* 6 bagels

---

¼ cup warm water

1 Tbsp. raw honey

1 packet active dry yeast

1½ cups blanched almond flour

½ cup flax meal

1 Tbsp. coconut flour

1 tsp. baking soda

½ tsp. sea salt, divided

5 eggs

2 Tbsp. apple cider vinegar

2 tsp. poppy seeds

1 Tbsp. toasted sesame seeds

1 Tbsp. dried garlic

---

1) Preheat the oven to 350°F. Lightly grease a bagel pan with coconut oil. In a small bowl, combine the warm water, honey, and yeast. Mix carefully with a fork. Set aside for 5 minutes, until foamy.

2) Combine the almond flour, flax meal, coconut flour, baking soda, and sea salt in a food processor. Pulse until smooth. Add the eggs, vinegar, and yeast mixture. Pulse until smooth.

3) Use a pastry bag to fill each bagel tin with batter. Smooth the tops.

4) In a small bowl, combine the poppy seeds, sesame seeds, dried garlic, and sea salt. Sprinkle the poppy seed mixture over the tops of the bagels. Bake for 20–25 minutes until golden. Enjoy!

GRANOLA BARS

These granola bars make the perfect on-the-go snack, to power your day with real food energy. My first recipe for granola bars became quite a hit on my blog, RealHealthyRecipes.com. However, I received requests for a sturdier version with the same great taste. Apparently, my granola bars were falling apart! Not cool. So you'll be excited to know that this new-and-improved granola bar recipe is super-duper sturdy and is just as tasty. Not that you were worried about taste; just look at them. Clearly they taste good.

Quick Tip: Repeat after me: "Keep calm and ignore junk food." This concept may be easier said than done, but trust me, it's quite possible to eliminate packaged junk from your life. Here's how:

Raid your pantry. Raid your freezer. Raid your junk food drawer. Raid the stash under your bed and in your glove compartment. Get. It. All. Out. Put all the junk food in a big garbage bag. Now get it out of your sight.

Keep it clean. Now that your life and home are cleared of junk food, keep it that way. Resist the urge to buy any more. Talk to your loved ones about keeping only wholesome food at home.

Find wholesome replacements for your old junk food faves and carry these with you. You know better than anyone what triggers you to fall off the clean eating wagon. Maybe it's the vending machine at work, or the fast food joint on your way home. Keep healthy food with you in order to avoid falling into old, bad habits.

Do you love packaged, sweet granola bars? Try this wholesome version instead!

Prep: 20 minutes ❋ *Bake:* 25 minutes ❋ *Oven:* 325°F ❋ *Makes:* 20 bars

---

2 Tbsp. milled chia seeds

2 Tbsp. flax meal

¼ cup water

½ cup raw pumpkin seeds

1 cup sliced almonds

⅓ cup + 1 Tbsp. coconut oil, divided

¼ cup honey

⅓ cup almond butter

¼ tsp. almond extract

2 cups unsweetened, shredded coconut

½ cup blanched almond flour

1 tsp. baking soda

1 Tbsp. sesame seeds

1 cup mini chocolate chips, divided

---

1) Preheat the oven to 325°F. Line an 8 × 8 pan with parchment paper.

2) In a small bowl, combine the milled chia seeds, flax meal, and water. Whisk with a fork and set aside for 5 minutes to thicken.

3) Place the pumpkin seeds and sliced almonds in a food processor. Pulse for 20 seconds. Add the coconut oil, honey, almond butter, and almond extract. Pulse for 20 seconds. Add the shredded coconut, almond flour, baking soda, and sesame seeds. Pulse until well combined. Add the mini chocolate chips. Use a large spoon to mix the chocolate chips into the dough.

4) Press the dough into the prepared pan. Smooth out the top. Bake for 20–25 minutes, until golden and bubbly. Remove from the oven and allow to cool in the pan for 15 minutes. Once cooled, loosen the sides with a knife, and then invert onto a cutting board. Remove the parchment paper by peeling off carefully. Cut into bars.

5) Combine the remaining 1 tablespoon coconut oil and ½ cup mini chocolate chips in a small pot. Place in a medium skillet of water and set over medium heat. Mix until smooth. Dip the bars into the melted chocolate and drizzle over the tops. Chill for 20 minutes to harden the chocolate. Enjoy!

GRANOLA

Move over Wheaties—a bowl of this crunchy granola, topped with chilled coconut milk and a handful of berries is truly the breakfast of champions. The concept of granola without oats may be a new one for you, but give it a try. The nuts and seeds that make up this granola are gluten and grain-free, but not flavor free. Oh yes, it has loads and loads of flavor.

Quick Tip: Save your homemade granola in an airtight container in the fridge for maximum freshness. You could also put a pretty bow on a nice glass jar full and give it away as a delicious, gluten-free gift. Wow, what a good friend you are.

Prep: 20 minutes ✹ *Bake:* 40 minutes ✹ *Oven:* 300°F ✹ *Makes:* 12 servings

1 cup raw pumpkin seeds
1 cup raw almonds
1 cup raw pecans
1 cup raw walnuts
3 Tbsp. coconut oil
¼ cup raw honey
1 Tbsp. vanilla extract
½ tsp. almond extract
2 Tbsp. flax meal
2 Tbsp. milled chia seeds
2 tsp. ground cinnamon
½ cup golden raisins
½ tsp. sea salt
½ cup sliced almonds

1) Preheat the oven to 300°F. Line a baking sheet with parchment paper.

2) Place the pumpkin seeds, almonds, pecans, and walnuts in a large bowl and cover with water. Soak for an hour. Drain and pat dry.

3) Combine the coconut oil, honey, vanilla extract, almond extract, flax meal, milled chia, cinnamon, golden raisins, and sea salt in a food processor. Pulse for 30–60 seconds, until the mixture reaches an even, granola-like consistency. Mix the sliced almonds into the mixture with a spoon.

4) Spread the granola mixture evenly over the prepared baking sheet. Bake for 10 minutes. Use a spoon to mix the granola up, and then bake for another 10 minutes. Continue to bake in 5 minute increments, stirring after each increment. Once your granola is crunchy and golden, remove it from the oven.

5) Store your granola in a glass jar in the fridge. Serve with chilled, unsweetened coconut milk and berries. Enjoy!

Keuilian

HOT CEREAL

When I was growing up, hot cereal could mean either oatmeal or cream of wheat. Both were eaten often, topped with brown sugar and milk. Since eliminating grains from my kitchen, I wanted to come up with a nutritious breakfast recipe that had the look and feel of hot cereal, without the grains and refined sugar. This combination of nuts and seeds is filled with fiber and is loaded with vitamins and minerals. Oh, and it's tasty too.

Quick Tip: The flax meal and milled chia seeds work to hold this cereal together. Both take a few minutes to get their bind on, so let your cereal sit for a few minutes and it will thicken up.

Prep: 10 minutes ❂ *Cook:* 0 minutes ❂ *Makes:* 4 servings

---

2 cups water

¼ cup raw pumpkin seeds

¼ cup raw walnuts

¼ cup unsweetened shredded coconut

½ cup golden flax meal

1 Tbsp. milled chia seeds

2 Tbsp. coconut palm sugar

1 tsp. ground cinnamon

¼ tsp. sea salt

Optional Toppings: chopped apple, raisins, sliced almonds, ground cinnamon, coconut palm sugar, and sea salt

---

1) Bring the water to a boil.

2) Combine the pepitas, walnuts, coconut, flax, chia, coconut palm sugar, cinnamon, and sea salt in a high-speed blender or food processor. Blend until a fine powder forms. Slowly pour in the boiling water. Continue to blend until smooth. Pour into individual serving bowls.

3) Sprinkle your favorite toppings on top of the warm hot cereal. If you're feeling a little crazy, douse your hot cereal with chilled coconut milk and a sprinkle of coconut palm sugar—that's what I do. Enjoy!

SWEET POTATO EGG CUPS

There's a popular recipe floating around on the Internet that takes frozen, shredded hash browns and cooks them in muffin cups with an egg on top. There's also butter and cheese involved. It looked pretty tasty, so I set out to create a more wholesome version. This recipe takes grated sweet potatoes and bakes an egg into it. The kids love this as an on-the-go breakfast—it's one of Andrew's standing breakfast requests!

Quick Tip: 1. Drink more water. 2. Eat more greens. 3. Say no to sugar. 4. Repeat.

Prep: 20 minutes ✸ *Bake:* 40 minutes ✸ *Oven:* 400°F ✸ *Makes:* 12 Servings

---

3 sweet potatoes
½ cup coconut oil, divided
sea salt and black pepper
12 eggs

---

1) Preheat the oven to 400°F. Lightly grease 12 muffin cups with coconut oil.

2) Scrub the sweet potatoes and place in a baking pan. Rub with coconut oil and season with salt and pepper. Bake for 25 minutes, until semi-tender.

3) Once the sweet potatoes are cool enough to handle, peel the skin, leaving just enough skin to grip one end. Use a cheese grater to shred the sweet potato. Place the shredded sweet potato in a medium bowl. Season with salt and pepper.

4) Press the shredded sweet potato mixture into each of the 12 muffin cups. Lightly brush with melted coconut oil. Bake for 15 minutes.

5) Crack an egg into each sweet potato cup. Season with sea salt and black pepper. Bake for another 10 minutes. Enjoy!

FRIED GREEN TOMATO BREAKFAST SANDWICH

Fried green tomatoes make me think of feel good, '90s chick flicks. And that makes me smile. This delectable breakfast sandwich also makes me smile. Who would have thought to create a bread-free breakfast sandwich with faux fried green tomatoes? This gal, that's who.

P.S. These tomatoes are also fantastic as a side dish with dinner—sans egg and bacon.

Quick Tip: Fried green tomatoes can also be baked rather than pan-fried. Preheat the oven to 400°F. In step 6, place the battered tomatoes on a parchment paper-lined baking sheet. Bake for 8 minutes, and then put under high broil for a minute or so, watching closely.

Prep: 25 minutes ❁ *Cook:* 20 minutes ❁ *Makes:* 4 servings

6 eggs, divided

½ cup canned coconut milk, full fat

⅓ cup coconut flour

½ tsp. sea salt

dash of black pepper

½ cup flax meal

3 Tbsp. coconut oil, divided

3 green heirloom tomatoes

4 slices bacon

1) In a shallow bowl, combine the eggs and coconut milk. Mix well.

2) In another shallow bowl, combine the coconut flour, sea salt, and black pepper.

3) In a third shallow bowl, place the flax meal.

4) Place a large skillet over medium-high heat and add 1 tablespoon coconut oil. Arrange the 3 shallow bowls together near the preheating skillet.

5) Slice the tomatoes to create 8 similarly-sized slices. Dip each slice of tomato first in the flour mixture. Carefully coat each side of the tomato slice with flour. Dip the flour-coated tomato slice in the egg mixture. Next, fully coat the tomato slice with flax meal.

6) Place the breaded tomato slice in the preheated pan. Cook each side for about 5 minutes, until golden. Set the cooked tomatoes aside.

7) Individually cook 4 eggs in a small skillet. Cook 4 slices of bacon in a skillet or in the oven until crispy. Assemble your breakfast sandwiches by stacking an egg and bacon between 2 tomato slices. Enjoy!

ROASTED PEPPER SAUSAGE

This easy-to-make sausage has real, authentic sausage flavor without the chemicals and preservatives of store-bought sausage. I love adding little bursts of flavor to homemade sausage patties, like the roasted pepper in this recipe. Sometimes I get a little wild and add diced cooked apples. Don't you love getting wild in the kitchen? Me too.

Quick Tip: No more excuses! Eat right today. Starting with a breakfast of protein-packed roasted pepper sausage. Beginning your day with a nutritious, low sugar breakfast will set you up for wise food decisions all day long.

Prep: 10 minutes ❁ *Cook:* 8 minutes ❁ *Makes:* 12 servings

2 tsp. sea salt

2 tsp. black pepper

2 tsp. dried oregano

2 tsp. dried thyme

2 tsp. ground sage

1 Tbsp. ground fennel

⅛ tsp. ground chili pepper

2 Tbsp. roasted red pepper, minced

2 lb. ground pork

1 Tbsp. coconut oil

1) Combine all of the ingredients, except the coconut oil, in a large bowl. Mix well with your hands— but wash them first! Form 12 sausage patties.

2) Heat the coconut oil in a large skillet over medium high heat. Cook the sausages until browned on both sides. Enjoy!

GREEN SMOOTHIE

I love how it feels to drink greens. There is magic in dark leafy things and this green smoothie is my magical elixir.

Back when I was a raw vegan (Gasp! Sigh. Yes, that was an interesting 2 years.) I would fill my son's sippy cup with green smoothie each morning for the drive to preschool. He was such a good sport about it. I think it helped that I would give him a quarter for each full cup of greens he drank. Heehee, bribery works.

Quick Tip: You may be tempted to leave out the wheatgrass—don't do it! The wheatgrass is this tasty smoothie's secret sauce. It's also highly nutritious and packed with vitamins and minerals. Which ones? The green ones.

Prep: 5 minutes ❁ *Makes:* 2 servings

1 cup coconut water

1 Tbsp. almond butter

¼ cup wheatgrass

2 cups fresh spinach

1 scoop high-quality, low carb chocolate protein

1 (1-inch) slice banana

½ cup ice

pinch of stevia (optional)

1) Cram all of the ingredients into a high-speed blender and have faith. Blend on high until the tiny pieces of spinach disappear. This can take a few minutes. Once the smoothie turns a brilliant shade of green, it's good to go. Wear that green moustache with pride. :)

GREEN CLEANSE JUICE

Something magical happens when you drink a cup of freshly made veggie juice, especially when it contains a generous helping of fresh ginger. It's as if your cells start to buzz! It's energizing and refreshing. And I've noticed an added benefit: it seems to act as a mild appetite suppressant. Bonus!

Quick Tip: Play around with the ingredients to find the very best flavor for you. I happen to really like ginger, so my version is usually quite spicy! If you are making this for the kids, feel free to add some chopped melon to sweeten it up.

Prep.: 5 minutes ✺ *Makes.:* 4 servings

---

1 bunch organic kale
1 bunch spinach
2 small green apples
4 large carrots
1 inch ginger root

---

1) Wash all of the ingredients. Quarter the apples.

2) Run everything through a juicer. Mix and drink immediately. Enjoy!

APPETIZERS

. . . that get the party started

ONION RINGS

Does this recipe even need an introduction? It's onion rings, people! Onion. Rings. And these ones haven't been battered in gluten and fried in lard. No, these ones are grain-free and baked, yet they taste just as finger-licking-good as the corner pub variety. Minus the bellyache. You're welcome.

Quick Tip: Why do we eat healthier versions of our favorite foods? Yes, it takes longer. Yes, it can be a hassle. Yes, it even costs more. But in the end our bodies are healthier, we have more energy, and we feel the magical synergy of real foods.

Prep: 25 minutes ❂ *Bake:* 20 minutes ❂ *Oven:* 450°F ❂ *Makes:* 4 servings

---

½ cup coconut flour

¼ tsp. garlic powder

4 tsp. sea salt, divided

1 (13.66-oz.) can coconut milk, full fat

4 eggs

1 cup ground almonds

1 cup flax meal

4 Tbsp. olive oil

2 large yellow onions

---

1) Preheat the oven to 450°F. Line a baking sheet with parchment paper.

2) In a shallow bowl, combine the coconut flour, garlic powder, and 2 teaspoons of sea salt.

3) In another shallow bowl, combine the coconut milk and eggs.

4) Take a large spoonful of the coconut flour mixture and whisk it into the egg mixture.

5) In a third shallow bowl, combine the ground almonds, flax meal, and olive oil.

6) Line the shallow bowls up together, with your prepared baking pan within arm's reach. Dredge the onion rings in the coconut flour mixture. Take the onion ring from the coconut flour mixture and dip it into the egg mixture. Take the onion ring from the egg mixture and dip it into the ground almond mixture.

7) Place the coated onion rings on the prepared baking sheet. Bake for 10 minutes, flip the onion rings, and bake for an additional 10 minutes. Serve with ketchup. Enjoy!

TORTILLA CHIPS

This recipe was a no-brainer. Let's see, we have awesome Coconut Flour Tortillas, we have fresh salsa . . . eureka! We shall make Tortilla Chips!

Quick Tip: Another wholesome alternative to traditional tortilla chips is to peel and slice fresh jicama into chip-sized pieces and dip in fresh guacamole. When you are out to eat at a Mexican restaurant, tell them to hold the chip basket and to bring out fresh veggies to dip into guacamole instead. Every single time I've requested this the restaurant has been able to make it happen. You may get a strange look from your waiter, but it's worth it!

Prep: 5 minutes ✸ *Bake:* 12 minutes ✸ *Oven:* 350°F ✸ *Makes:* 4 servings

---

5 Coconut Flour Tortillas (page 144)

olive oil

sea salt

---

1) Preheat the oven to 350°F.

2) Cut each tortilla into 4 wedges. Rub the tortilla wedges with olive oil and sprinkle with sea salt. Spread across a rimmed baking sheet.

3) Bake for 6 minutes, flip and bake for another 6 minutes. For extra crispy chips, place under the high broil for 1–2 minutes, watching very closely so it doesn't burn. Serve with fresh salsa and guacamole. Enjoy!

ZUCCHINI STICKS

There are so many amazing recipes to be made with zucchini. From brownies to pasta to crispy zucchini sticks—what a versatile vegetable! These zucchini sticks are a very popular snack in my house. The kids start in on them while they're still hot from the oven. Needless to say, these don't last long!

Quick Tip: The key to very crispy zucchini sticks, without the use of a fryer, is to salt the zucchini and drain excess liquid before baking. While this step does take an hour, the result is quite worth it.

Prep: 1 hour 20 minutes ❂ *Bake:* 20 minutes ❂ *Oven:* 425°F ❂ *Makes:* 4 servings

---

3 zucchini

1 Tbsp. sea salt

2 Tbsp. coconut flour

¼ tsp. garlic powder

2 eggs

¼ cup canned coconut milk, full fat

½ cup blanched almond flour

½ cup flax meal

⅓ cup nutritional yeast

1 Tbsp. dried oregano

Lazy Man's Ranch (page 160)

---

1) Preheat the oven to 425°F. Line a baking sheet with parchment paper.

2) Cut each zucchini in half, horizontally, and then make 2 cuts in each direction to create 9 sticks. Place the zucchini sticks in a colander and sprinkle with salt. Set in a sink and allow to drain for 1 hour. After an hour, you'll see beads of liquid on the zucchini. Rinse with cold water. Pat the zucchini sticks dry.

3) In a shallow bowl, combine the coconut flour and garlic powder.

4) In another shallow bowl, combine the eggs and coconut milk.

5) Transfer 1 tablespoon of the egg mixture into the coconut flour mixture. Whisk to create a paste.

6) In a third shallow bowl, combine the blanched almond flour, flax meal, nutritional yeast, and dried oregano.

7) Arrange the 3 bowls close together, with the prepared baking sheet within arms reach. First rub the zucchini sticks in the coconut flour paste. Then dip in the egg mixture. Finally sprinkle with the nutritional yeast mixture.

8) Place the coated zucchini sticks on the prepared baking sheet. Bake for 12 minutes, flip, and bake for another 12 minutes. Turn the broiler on high for a minute or two to brown. Remove from the oven and serve with Lazy Man's Ranch. Enjoy!

SWEET POTATO FRIES WITH MAPLE DIP

My friend, Cara, and I are slightly obsessed with sweet potato fries and, well, fries in general. Recently we dined with a group of friends in a quaint patio restaurant at a winery in Temecula, where duck fat fries were the specialty. Naturally we wanted to sample all of the flavors on the menu . . . and there were seven flavors. It was only slightly embarrassing when the manager came out to take our picture. Apparently we were the first people in history to order all the flavors at once!

As much as I love eating real fries on cheat days, these baked sweet potato fries taste just as good as the greasy ones. And with these ones you get to avoid the fry-induced bellyache.

Quick Tip: These fries could also be made spicy, rather than cinnamon-y. To do so, simply replace the cinnamon with ¼ teaspoon ground cumin and ¼ teaspoon chili powder. Serve with Lazy Man's Ranch (page 160) instead of the Maple Dip.

Prep: 20 minutes ✿ *Bake:* 15 minutes ✿ *Oven:* 400°F ✿ *Makes:* 4 servings

---

2 sweet potatoes

1 Tbsp. arrowroot starch

1 Tbsp. coconut oil

1 Tbsp. coconut palm sugar

½ tsp. sea salt

1 tsp. ground cinnamon

1 (13.66-oz.) can coconut milk, full fat (chilled overnight)

2 Tbsp. pure maple syrup

---

1) Preheat the oven to 400°F. Line a baking sheet with parchment paper.

2) Use a vegetable peeler to skin the sweet potatoes. Cut into french fry-size pieces. Place the fries in a large ziploc bag and dump in the arrowroot starch. Close the bag and shake until evenly coated. Sprinkle the coconut oil, coconut palm sugar, sea salt, and cinnamon over the fries in the bag. Close the bag and shake until evenly coated.

3) Spread the fries over the prepared baking sheet. Bake for 15 minutes.

4) Combine the coconut cream and maple syrup in a small bowl. Chill for 15 minutes. Enjoy!

SWEET POTATO SKINS

Warning: these sweet potato skins are dangerously delicious! Perfect for serving as an appetizer or a game day snack, this recipe is quite the crowd pleaser. You won't believe it's dairy-free.

Quick Tip: Often times the sweet potatoes you find at the market are huge. For this recipe it's important to seek out the itty-bitty sweet potatoes at the bottom of the pile.

Prep: 20 minutes ✿ *Bake:* 45–55 minutes ✿ *Oven:* 400°F ✿ *Makes:* 8 servings

---

4 small sweet potatoes
6 Tbsp. coconut oil, divided
3 slices nitrate-free bacon, cooked
3 green onions
1 cup Dairy-Free Cheese Spread (page 166)
½ cup Lazy Man's Ranch (page 160)

---

1) Preheat the oven to 400°F. Brush the sweet potatoes with melted coconut oil. Place on a lightly greased baking sheet. Bake for 30–40 minutes, until fork tender.

2) Once cooled, slice the sweet potatoes in half, lengthwise. Use an ice cream scooper to scoop out most of the sweet potato flesh. Use the tender sweet potato for something awesome, like whipped sweet potatoes.

3) Place the scooped sweet potato skins back on the baking sheet. Brush with melted coconut oil. Bake, bottoms up, for 5 minutes. Turn over and bake for another 5 minutes.

4) Fill each sweet potato with Dairy-Free Cheese Spread (page 166) and top with chopped bacon. Bake for another 5 minutes. Top with Lazy Man's Ranch (page 160) and chopped green onions. Enjoy!

BACON-WRAPPED PEPPERS

Oh my goodness. These are crazy good. And I'm not just saying that because I invented them. Well, I didn't invent the entire concept of bacon-wrapped peppers, just the idea of stuffing them with dairy-free cashew cheese. To be completely honest with you, I don't like sharing these. They're just too delicious to share. Make a batch for yourself and a batch to share. There we go—compromise.

Quick Tip: Save yourself some pain by wearing gloves while chopping the jalapeños. If my lazy chef ways have rubbed off on you, then you might be tempted to skip the gloves anyway. Just be prepared to feel some burning in your hands from the contact with the peppers. Ten different people will give you ten different ways to relieve the burning—from olive oil to Vaseline. I find that squeezing fresh lemon juice over the burning skin offers some relief. Just wear the gloves.

Prep: 25 minutes ❂ *Bake*: 27 minutes ❂ *Oven*: 375°F ❂ *Makes*: 24 peppers

---

12 peppers, jalapeños or sweet peppers (or a mixture of both!)

½ cup Dairy-Free Cheese Spread (page 166)

12 nitrate-free bacon slices, cut in half

24 toothpicks

---

1) Preheat the oven to 375°F. Line a baking sheet with parchment paper.

2) Slice the peppers in half, lengthwise. Scoop out and discard the seeds. Fill each pepper half with Dairy-Free Cheese Spread.

3) Wrap each pepper half with a slice of bacon. Secure with a toothpick.

4) Place the wrapped peppers in a single layer on the prepared baking pan. Bake for 20–25 minutes, and then place under the broiler on high for 2 minutes, until lightly browned. Enjoy!

BLT BITES

I'm obsessive about putting out snacks and appetizers when we have people over. If my guests don't have something to eat, then the world is going to end. Before I started eating healthy, I would put out appetizers that were greasy and smothered in cheese. Sure, these tasted good, but my guests deserve more than simply good taste. They deserve an appetizer that is going to taste good and make them feel good. Like these adorable BLT Bites.

Quick Tip: Make these BLT Bites a few hours before your guests arrive. Store on the serving tray in your fridge, and simply pull it out when you're ready to make some people very, very happy.

Prep: 20 minutes ❁ *Makes:* 24 bites

---

12 cherry tomatoes

3 slices nitrate-free bacon, cooked and crumbled

½ cup Lazy Man's Ranch (page 160)

2 green onions, finely chopped

2 Tbsp. fresh parsley, minced

---

1) Cut each tomato in half and gently scoop out the insides with a spoon. Place the tomato halves cut side-down and allow to drain for 10 minutes.

2) Mix the bacon, ranch, onions, and parsley in a small bowl. Spoon into the tomato halves. Chill for 15 minutes or until ready to serve. Enjoy!

WRAPPED ASPARAGUS

Best. Appetizer. Ever. There's not much else to say about these teriyaki spiked, tender, rib eye-wrapped asparagi. Asparaguses? Asparagee? Anyway, when you are looking for an appetizer or side dish that is truly flavorful and addictive, look no further than this page.

Quick Tip: I find these wraps to be just as delicious when served chilled as they are when served hot. If you're making these for guests, it's nice to make them ahead of time and chill them on the serving platter. Just don't start "taste-testing," or you may end up with an empty platter.

Prep: 1 hour 25 minutes ✿ *Cook:* 20 minutes ✿ *Makes:* 4 servings

½ cup sake

½ cup mirin

½ cup coconut aminos

2 Tbsp. pure maple syrup

2 Tbsp. minced fresh ginger

2 Tbsp. minced fresh garlic

1 lb. thinly sliced rib eye (see quick tip on page 104)

1 bunch asparagus

sea salt

1 lemon, juice and zest

black pepper

1 Tbsp. sesame oil

1) Combine the sake, mirin, coconut aminos, syrup, ginger, and garlic in a bowl. Mix well.

2) Arrange the sliced rib eye in a shallow pan. Pour the marinade over the rib eye. Place in the fridge to marinate for an hour.

3) Bring a large pot of water to boil. Add a sprinkle of sea salt. Wash the asparagus and trim the tough ends. Add the asparagus to the boiling water. Blanch for about 10 minutes, until tender and vibrantly green. Drain.

4) Place the blanched asparagus in a medium bowl. Combine with the lemon, lemon zest, pepper, and sesame oil.

5) Wrap each blanched asparagus with a piece of marinated rib eye. Place back in the shallow pan. Spoon the marinade over the wraps. At this point you could keep the wraps in the fridge for up to a few hours, until you are ready to cook.

6) Place a large skillet over medium-high heat. Add the wrapped asparagus to the preheated skillet and cook until browned, about 5 minutes per side. Enjoy!

EASY BAKED MEATBALLS

Have you noticed how almost all snack foods are bad for you?

It's like there's a law that anything quick and easy to grab has to be filled with carbohydrates or straight up sugar. Until now.

These easy baked meatballs are the perfect, anti high-carb snack to enjoy on a busy afternoon. This is also makes for a healthy, quick week-night dinner.

Quick Tip: Most meatball recipes call for breadcrumbs, which adds gluten and carbs to an otherwise protein-packed snack. I've found that blanched almond flour works as a low-carb, gluten-free substitute for the breadcrumbs in these recipes. If a meatball recipe calls for ½ cup of breadcrumbs, replace it with ¼ cup blanched almond flour.

Prep: 20 minutes ❁ *Bake:* 30 minutes ❁ *Oven:* 425°F ❁ *Makes:* 40 meatballs

---

1 Tbsp. coconut oil

2 celery sticks, finely minced

2 carrots, finely minced

1 small yellow onion, finely minced

¼ cup pecans, finely minced

½ cup fresh parsley, finely minced

2 cloves garlic, finely minced

½ tsp. sea salt

½ tsp. ground fennel

¼ tsp. ground sage

¼ tsp. onion powder

¼ tsp. garlic powder

dash of black pepper

2 lb. ground pork

---

1) Preheat the oven to 425°F. Lightly grease a large baking pan with coconut oil.

2) Place the coconut oil in a large skillet. Add the chopped celery, carrots, onion, pecans, and parsley. Cook for about 5 minutes, until soft.

3) Combine the ground pork with all of the gathered spices. Mix well with your hands. Add the cooked vegetables. Mix in and form 40 meatballs.

4) Place the meatballs in the prepared baking pan. Bake for 30 minutes, until cooked through. Enjoy!

PULLED PORK SANDWICHES

I love a good slow cooker recipe, and this one is in my top 5. It feels almost too easy, since the time you invest is about 10 minutes, and then dinner turns out amazingly tender and savory. This recipe is way too good not to try, so what are you waiting for?

Quick Tip: You could easily serve this pulled pork on large lettuce leaves rather than Fluffy Egg White Biscuits. It's delicious both ways!

Prep: 5 minutes ❁ *Cook:* 5½ hours ❁ *Makes:* 12 servings

---

1 tsp. olive oil

1 cup BBQ Sauce + more for serving (page 168)

½ cup apple cider vinegar

1 Tbsp. Dijon mustard

1 Tbsp. chili powder

1 large onion, chopped

3 garlic cloves, minced

2 tsp. dried thyme

½ cup chicken broth

4 lb. pork shoulder roast

Fluffy Egg White Biscuits (page 154)

---

1) Combine the olive oil, BBQ Sauce, vinegar, Dijon, chili powder, onion, garlic cloves, dried thyme, and chicken broth in a bowl.

2) Place the shoulder roast in a slow cooker. Cover the roast with the BBQ Sauce mixture. Cover and cook on high for 5½ hours.

3) Remove the pork from the slow cooker. Gather a plate and 2 clean forks. Use the forks to shred the tender pork and separate and discard pieces of fat. Assemble sandwiches with shredded pork and BBQ Sauce. Enjoy!

CHICKEN LETTUCE BOATS

These Chicken Lettuce Boats are both pretty and refreshing. I like to serve these chilled on a warm summer's afternoon. The creamy coconut dressing combined with crunchy grapes and celery and tender chicken make for a memorable bite.

Quick Tip: Do you have leftover chicken breast from last night's dinner? This recipe is the perfect way to breath new life into day-old, cooked chicken.

Prep: 25 minutes ✿ *Makes:* 6 servings

---

1 (13.66-oz.) can coconut milk, full fat

¼ cup chopped fresh cilantro

1 Tbsp. apple cider vinegar

1 Tbsp. coconut oil

⅛ tsp. garlic powder

zest from 1 small lemon

1 tsp. lemon juice

dash of sea salt

dash of black pepper

1 cup finely chopped celery

1 cup finely chopped red grapes

½ cup finely chopped raw pecans

1 green apple, finely chopped

1 (4-oz.) can mild green chiles, finely chopped

1 lb. roasted chicken

5 heads endive

---

1) Combine the coconut milk, cilantro, vinegar, coconut oil, garlic powder, lemon zest, lemon juice, sea salt, and black pepper in a bowl. Mix well.

2) Combine the celery, grapes, pecans, apple, chiles, and chicken in a large bowl. Pour the cream sauce over the chicken mixture and mix well. Spoon the chicken mixture into endive cups. Enjoy!

PRETZEL BITES

Warm, doughy pretzel bites are my idea of comfort food. Add a side of tangy sweet mustard and I'm in heaven. These soft, salty morsels do not last long around my house. It's a mysterious disappearing act. One minute I have a bowl of pretzel bites, fresh from the oven, and the next there's nothing but a little pile of crumbs. Very curious . . .

Quick Tip: Sprinkle the coarse salt quickly after brushing the egg mixture on each pretzel bite to make sure that lots of yummy salt sticks to the dough. Also don't skip the broiling step—make the tops of those pretzels nice and toasty. But not too toasty. Burnt pretzels aren't quite as tasty.

Prep: 25 minutes ❀ *Bake:* 20 minutes ❀ *Oven:* 400°F ❀ *Makes:* 4 servings

---

½ cup filtered water

½ cup coconut oil

2 Tbsp. apple cider vinegar

2 eggs, divided

½ tsp. sea salt

½ cup arrowroot starch, plus more for dusting

½ tsp. baking soda

½ tsp. baking powder

⅔ cup coconut flour

½ cup blanched almond flour

3 Tbsp. coarse salt

⅓ cup stone ground mustard

2 Tbsp. raw honey

---

1) Preheat the oven to 400°F. Line a baking sheet with parchment paper.

2) Combine the water, coconut oil, vinegar, and one egg in a bowl. Mix well.

3) Combine the sea salt, arrowroot starch, baking soda, baking powder, coconut flour, and almond flour in another bowl. Mix well. Add the dry ingredients to the wet ingredients and mix well to form dough.

4) Dust a cutting board and your hands with arrowroot starch. This will prevent the dough from sticking. Carefully roll 6–8 snakes with the dough. Use a knife to cut the rolls into 1–2 inch pieces. Carefully mold each piece of dough into the shape of a pretzel bite and place on the prepared pan. Don't worry about making each bite identical—it's all going to taste delicious. Bake for 15 minutes in the preheated oven.

5) Whisk the egg in a small bowl with a fork. Brush the tops of each pretzel bite with the egg mixture and sprinkle with coarse salt. Return the pretzel bites to the oven for 5 minutes.

6) Turn the broiler on high for a minute to brown the tops. Watch closely, because these puppies can burn quickly if left too long under the broil. An even, golden brown is what you want.

7) Gather the stone ground mustard and raw honey. Combine together to create a tangy-sweet dip. Enjoy!

ROASTED ONION DIP

Kiss your old sour cream-based dips goodbye. Kick them to the curb. Tell them to pack their bags and hit the road. You've got this phenomenal roasted onion dip now and it's not going to disappoint. It's dairy-free and flavorful. In the words of Michael Scott: You won't regret this.

Quick Tip: Start making small improvements to your diet, then work your way to a larger goal. First replace that sour cream dip with this Roasted Onion Dip. Then replace those chips with roasted or fresh veggies. Look, you're still munching and dipping, you've simply improved the quality of the munch and dip. You get what I'm saying?

Prep: 30 minutes ❀ *Cook:* 40 minutes ❀ *Oven:* 380°F ❀ *Makes:* 1 cup

---

1 yellow onion, sliced

1 Tbsp. coconut oil

2 Tbsp. apple cider vinegar

2 Tbsp. raw honey

1 Tbsp. Dijon mustard

¼ tsp. sea salt

1 cup raw cashews

assorted veggies: asparagus, carrots, parsnips, radishes, and turnips

sweet paprika (for garnish)

pumpkin seeds (for garnish)

---

1) Preheat the oven to 380 degrees. Lightly grease a rimmed baking sheet with coconut oil.

2) Place the coconut oil and onion in a skillet. Place over low heat, stirring occasionally for 20 minutes, until caramelized. Once the onions have caramelized, remove from heat.

3) Soak the cashews in hot water for 10 minutes. Discard the water.

4) Combine the onions, cashews, vinegar, honey, and salt in a food processor. Blend until smooth.

5) Wash and trim the veggies. Place on the prepared baking sheet. Roast for 40–60 minutes. Serve the roasted veggies with the dip. Enjoy!

CREAMY FRUIT DIP

I had a lot of fun coming up with this recipe and it came out spoon-lickingly good. Most kids love to dip fruit slices into sugar-sweetened yogurt, so this recipe was my dairy-free, sugar-free version. It took a lot of self restraint to stop eating this dip long enough to snap a picture, and I ended up taking a few bites in between . . . heehee.

The genius of this recipe, in my opinion, is the freeze dried strawberries. I love using freeze dried fruit to create wholesome versions of kid-favorite treats because it's easy to pulse into a convenient powder, it has stunning natural color, and it contains natural sweetness, instead of processed sugar. If you love strawberry yogurt but can't stomach dairy and want to limit your sugar intake, give this recipe a try. It's super quick and really, really tasty.

Quick Tip: Another fun snack to make for the kids using freeze dried fruit is my wholesome recipe for Fun Dip. Peel and slice jicama into sticks. Grind 1 cup of freeze dried fruit in a food processor until it becomes a fine powder. Pour the dip into a individual bowls, or ziplock bags, and serve with a handful of jicama sticks for dipping and licking. Yum!

Prep: 5 minutes ❀ *Makes:* 4 servings

½ cup freeze dried strawberries
1 (13.66-oz.) can coconut milk, full fat
1 tsp. vanilla extract
2 ripe bananas
¼ tsp. almond extract
1 Tbsp. arrowroot starch
sliced fresh fruit for dipping

1) Combine all of the ingredients in a food processor. Blend until smooth. Chill before serving. Enjoy!

MAIN DISHES

. . . without the guilt

GROUND BEEF TACOS

Make-your-own-taco night is a very popular event at my house. The kids take their taco making very seriously, and provide commentary the whole way through. Chloe: My taco is very salad-y. More lettuce. More tomatoes. Andrew: Pass the beef, I missed a spot. Oh yeah, this thing is l-o-a-d-e-d!

Quick Tip: Make your tortillas the day before, or the morning of, to save yourself prep time right before dinner. The tortilla making is the most time-consuming part of this dinner, but the result is so delicious that it's worth it.

Prep: 15 minutes ✺ *Cook:* 10 minutes ✺ *Makes:* 4 servings

---

2 tsp. chili powder

½ tsp. sweet paprika

½ tsp. cumin

½ tsp. onion powder

¼ tsp. garlic powder

¼ tsp. sea salt

2 lb. grass-fed ground beef

12 Coconut Flour Tortillas (page 144)

Toppings: diced tomato, shredded lettuce,
sliced olives, guacamole, salsa, and pico de gallo

1) Combine the spices with the ground beef. Mix well. Go ahead and get your hands dirty. In a large skillet over medium-high heat, brown the beef.

2) Put the browned ground beef in a large bowl and set out with a stack of tortillas and taco toppings. Have fun assembling and devouring your tacos. Enjoy!

ENCHILADAS

When I set out to create an enchilada recipe that was gluten- and dairy-free, I'll admit that I was a little bit skeptical. I mean, isn't the whole appeal of enchiladas the tortilla smothered in melted cheese? Well, turns out tortillas and cheese are overrated. These dairy- and gluten-free enchiladas are more flavorful and satisfying than any traditional enchiladas I've tasted!

Quick Tip: To make sure the shredded chicken breast was extremely tender, I used a slow cooker. This is hands down my favorite way to cook chicken breast. However, if you're pressed for time, then cook the chicken breast in a skillet. Also, make the tortillas the day before to really cut down on prep time.

Prep: 30 minutes ❂ *Cook:* 20 minutes ❂ *Oven:* 350°F ❂ *Makes:* 12 servings

---

2 boneless, skinless chicken breasts

dash of sea salt and black pepper

2 tsp. fajita spice, divided

2 cups chicken broth

3 bell peppers

2 garlic cloves

1 yellow onion

1 Tbsp. olive oil

1 (8-oz.) can green chiles, chopped

1 tsp. ground cumin

12 Coconut Flour Tortillas (page 144)

1 (16-oz.) jar enchilada sauce

fresh cilantro, chopped

---

1) Rinse the chicken breasts and pat dry. Rub the chicken breasts with the sea salt, black pepper, and 1 teaspoon fajita spice. Place the chicken breast in a slow cooker. Cover with the chicken broth. Cover and cook on low for 6 hours. Remove the chicken breast from the slow cooker. Shred with a fork.

2) Slice the onion and bell peppers and mince the garlic. Place the olive oil in a large skillet over medium high heat. Add the sliced veggies and garlic. Add the green chiles, ground cumin, remaining 1 teaspoon fajita spice, and shredded chicken.

3) Preheat the oven to 350°F. Lightly grease a casserole pan with olive oil. Spread a spoonful of enchilada sauce on the bottom of the pan.

4) Fill a shallow bowl with enchilada sauce. Dip each tortilla in the sauce. Place ½ cup of the chicken filling in a line down the center of each tortilla. Wrap up and place in the pan. Continue with the remaining chicken filling and tortillas.

5) Bake, uncovered, for 20 minutes. Sprinkle with chopped cilantro and cover with more enchilada sauce. Enjoy!

PIZZA DOUGH

Pizza is one of the hardest things to give up when going grain- and gluten-free, so I say let's make a pizza dough without the grains. So you can give up grains and eat your pizza too!

I've hacked the code for grain-free pizza dough with this one. Cover it in Dairy-Free Cheese Spread and top it with all your favorite pizza toppings. Woop, woop!

Quick Tip: Sometimes I use actual yeast in this pizza dough recipe, just to give it that yeasty flavor. It's totally unnecessary for the functionality of the dough—just for flavor. To do so, mix the water (warm) with 1 packet (2 teaspoons) active dry yeast and 1 tablespoon raw honey. Mix well and let the mixture sit for 10 minutes. It should get big and foamy. Add the yeast mixture in step 3.

Prep: 20 minutes ✿ *Bake:* 8 minutes ✿ *Oven:* 425°F ✿ *Makes:* 1 pizza crust

---

¾ cup blanched almond flour

3 Tbsp. coconut flour

½ cup arrowroot starch

¼ tsp. sea salt

¼ cup water

1 egg

1 Tbsp. olive oil

1 tsp. apple cider vinegar

---

1) Preheat the oven to 425°F. Line a baking sheet with parchment paper.

2) Combine the almond flour, coconut flour, arrowroot starch, and sea salt in a bowl. Mix well.

3) Combine the water, egg, olive oil, and vinegar in another bowl. Add the wet ingredients to the dry ones. Mix and form into a dough ball. Wrap the dough in plastic wrap and chill for 15 minutes in the fridge.

4) Place the dough on a piece of parchment paper. Cover with another piece of parchment paper. Use a rolling pin to flatten the dough into a pizza crust shape. Or shape it into a heart. Or octagon—whatever floats your boat! Pinch the edges of the dough to form a crust. Place the dough and parchment paper on a baking sheet and bake for 8 minutes, until golden. Load up with your favorite toppings, bake for another 5 minutes, and then enjoy!

BBQ CHICKEN PIZZA

This BBQ Chicken Pizza is the perfect balance of tangy BBQ, tender chicken, spicy onion, and refreshing cilantro. You'll never want boring old pepperoni pizza again.

Quick Tip: I like to use the slow cooker to cook perfectly moist chicken breast for this pizza recipe. Season the chicken breast with sea salt, black pepper, and fajita spices. Place in a slow cooker and cover with chicken broth. Cover and cook on low for 6 hours. Shred the chicken and then mix with the BBQ sauce in step 2.

Prep: 25 minutes ❁ *Bake:* 5 minutes ❁ *Oven:* 425°F ❁ *Makes:* 1 pizza

---

1 red onion

⅓ cup fresh cilantro

1 cup roasted, shredded chicken

½ cup BBQ Sauce (page 168), divided

1 Pizza Dough crust (page 84)

½ cup Dairy-Free Cheese Spread (page 166)

---

1) Preheat the oven to 425°F. Line a baking sheet with parchment paper.

2) In a small bowl, combine the chicken with half of the BBQ sauce.

3) Arrange a pre-baked pizza crust on your prepared baking sheet. Spread the remaining BBQ sauce over the crust. Sprinkle Dairy-Free Cheese Spread over the pizza. Top with the sliced onions. Top with the BBQ chicken.

4) Bake for 5 minutes to brown the edges. Sprinkle with chopped cilantro. Enjoy!

LEEK AND SWEET POTATO PIZZA

This is my favorite pizza! The combination of tender leeks and sweet potatoes is crazy good. It's fun to make pizza with unusual toppings; it makes me feel fancy. Then I realize that there's leek on my face and I stop feeling fancy.

Quick Tip: Guess what? Crash diets don't work. I would know, since I tried them all before turning to a diet of simple, real, wholesome foods. Don't starve yourself. Don't drink chalky diet shakes. Don't experiment with diet pills or potions. Don't choke down meal replacement bars. Those products sell you hope, which feels nice, but in the end you're out some money and you're just as frustrated as before.

There is no diet that will do what eating healthy does. Skip the diet. Just eat real, wholesome food. Start with this leek and sweet potato pizza.

Prep: 25 minutes ❂ *Bake:* 5 minutes ❂ *Oven:* 425°F ❂ *Makes:* 1 pizza

---

1 sweet potato

1 leek

1 Tbsp. dried rosemary

black pepper

1 Tbsp. olive oil

½ cup Dairy-Free Cheese Spread (page 166)

1 Pizza Dough crust (page 84)

---

1) Preheat the oven to 425°F. Line a baking sheet with parchment paper.

2) Peel the sweet potato and thinly slice into half moons. Thinly slice the leek, discarding most of the green ends. Place the sweet potato and leek slices in a medium skillet in an inch of water. Bring the water to a boil and blanch until tender, about 5 minutes. Drain the water from the skillet. Sprinkle the rosemary, pepper, and olive oil over the cooked sweet potato and leek slices. Toss to evenly coat.

3) Arrange a pre-baked pizza crust on your prepared baking sheet. Spread the Dairy-Free Cheese Spread evenly over the crust. Use your fingers! Arrange the sweet potato slices over the pizza. Top with the tender leeks. Sprinkle with extra pepper and dried rosemary.

4) Bake for 5 minutes. Enjoy!

PEAR AND BALSAMIC PIZZA

Pear and balsamic vinegar make quite the flavor combination. It's tangy and sweet, all at the same time. Add to that the savory pizza dough and Dairy-Free Cheese Spread, and well, you've just taken me to flavor heaven. I'm going to stay awhile.

Quick Tip: Balsamic glaze is easy to make at home. Here's how: Bring 2 cups balsamic vinegar to a simmer in a saucepan. Turn the heat to low and reduce for about 40 minutes. The liquid should reduce down to about ½ cup. Use the glaze to dress up salads, veggies, meat dishes, and even drizzle over fresh fruit and Vanilla Ice Cream (page 210).

Prep: 25 minutes ❂ *Bake:* 5 minutes ❂ *Oven:* 425°F ❂ *Makes:* 1 pizza

---

¼ cup balsamic vinegar

2 Tbsp. coconut palm sugar

1 yellow onion

1 tsp. fresh thyme

2 Tbsp. olive oil

sprinkle of sea salt

1 pear

juice from ½ lemon

½ cup Dairy-Free Cheese Spread (page 166)

¼ cup pecans, chopped

1 Pizza Dough crust (page 84)

---

1) Preheat the oven to 425°F. Line a baking sheet with parchment paper.

2) Combine the balsamic vinegar and coconut palm sugar in a saucepan. Mix well. Bring to a simmer. Cook until the mixture becomes thick and syrupy—about 5 minutes.

3) Place the onion, thyme, and olive oil in a small skillet. Cook over medium heat until the onions are soft. Sprinkle the salt over the onions in the skillet. Cook for 2 more minutes then remove from heat.

4) Thinly slice the pear and sprinkle with the lemon juice.

5) Arrange a pre-baked pizza crust on your prepared baking sheet. Spread the Dairy-Free Cheese Spread evenly over the crust. Use your fingers! Top with the cooked thyme onions. Top with the sliced pears. Top with chopped pecans. Bake for 5 minutes.

6) Sprinkle with fresh thyme and a drizzle of the balsamic syrup. Enjoy!

FULLY LOADED BURGERS

Good eating habits are just as addictive as bad eating habits. This is true because that's all it is: a habit. If you're used to eating a burger with a big, spongy white bun then you'll eat it that way every single time. Likewise, if you're used to eating a burger wrapped in lettuce, then you'll eat it that way every single time. And the habit that involves lettuce rather than white buns is going to leave you a lot leaner and healthier. So why not?

Quick Tip: If ground beef is not your thing then make these luscious, fully loaded burgers using ground turkey or ground chicken breast. Or really treat yourself and use ground bison. Mmmmmmmm.

Prep: 20 minutes ❃ *Cook:* 15 minutes ❃ *Makes:* 6 burgers

1 yellow onion

1 Tbsp. olive oil

1 lb. organic ground beef

2 Tbsp. blanched almond flour

1 Tbsp. tomato paste

1 Tbsp. balsamic glaze

6 slices bacon

12 large lettuce leaves

3 tomatoes, sliced

¼ cup chives

1) Peel and slice the onion. Place the onion slices and olive oil in a skillet over medium high heat. Cook until the onions caramelize.

2) Combine the ground beef, almond flour, tomato paste, and balsamic glaze in a bowl. Form 6 patties. Grill to desired doneness.

3) Cook the bacon in a skillet or in the oven until crispy. Blot with a paper towel. Assemble the burgers with lettuce on the bottom and top, sliced tomato, bacon slices, caramelized onions, and a sprinkle of chopped chives. Enjoy!

QUINOA BURGERS

When I was 12 years old I stopped eating meat, literally cold turkey. I had been eating leftover turkey soup, and I put down my spoon and announced that meat just wasn't for me. For the next 18 years I didn't eat meat. Not even a bite. Until, at 30, I found myself frustrated with my attempts to eat a low-carb diet that didn't include meat. And, just like that, I started eating meat again. Beginning with a bite of cold turkey.

While I am quite happy with my current meat-eating ways, I have a few vegetarians in my life who are very dear to my heart. My younger brother, Pete, and his lovely wife, Betsy, are devout vegans; and my dear friend, Cara, is meat-free. These meat-free burgers were made for the special lettuce lovers in my life.

Quick Tip: If you are inclined to eat beans, then the cauliflower can be subbed out for 1 cup cooked black beans. Blend ½ cup beans in step 6 and then mix the remaining ½ cup in whole.

Prep: 25 minutes ❋ *Bake:* 40 minutes ❋ *Oven:* 375°F ❋ *Makes:* 6 burgers

---

6 Tbsp. water

2 Tbsp. flax meal

1 cup red quinoa

2 cups water or broth

1 head cauliflower, chopped into florets

½ cup yellow onion, chopped

1 Tbsp. olive oil

2 tsp. ground cumin

2 tsp. ground coriander

½ tsp. ground cayenne (or sweet paprika for a more mild flavor)

1 Tbsp. balsamic glaze

1 Tbsp. tomato paste

½ cup pecans, chopped

1 Tbsp. coconut aminos

large lettuce leaves

tomato slices

red onion slices

fresh sprouts

---

1) Preheat the oven to 375°F. Line a baking sheet with parchment paper.

2) Combine the water and flax meal in a bowl. Mix well. Let it sit for 5 minutes, to thicken.

3) Combine the quinoa and water or broth in a saucepan. Bring to a boil over medium-high heat. Reduce to a simmer, cover and cook for 20 minutes. Remove from heat and fluff.

4) Place the chopped cauliflower in a skillet with an inch of water. Bring to a boil and then reduce to a simmer for 10 minutes, or until the cauliflower is soft.

5) Heat the olive oil in a skillet over medium high heat. Add the onion and mix in the gathered spices. Cook until soft. Add the balsamic glaze, tomato paste, pecans, and coconut aminos to the skillet. Stir and cook for a few more minutes, and then remove from heat.

6) Combine the onion mixture, cooked cauliflower, and 1 cup of the cooked quinoa in a food processor along with the flax mixture. Pulse until combined. Place the remaining cook quinoa on a plate. Form patties and evenly coat with the quinoa.

7) Arrange the patties on the prepared baking sheet. Cook for 40 minutes, or until fully cooked. Arrange each burger on lettuce with slices of tomato, red onion and fresh sprouts. Enjoy!

TEX-MEX HOT DOGS

Do you know what traditional hot dogs are made of? This isn't a horror book so I don't want to be too graphic here. Let's just say the words mechanically separated, blended meat, bone bits, corn syrup, high sodium, preservatives, chemicals, artificial colors, as well as artificial flavors are involved. Enough said.

Feel free to enjoy these wholesome, homemade hot dogs with peace of mind. These dogs are made with a combination of cooked ham with ground pork that gives it an authentic hot dog taste, all without the frightening ingredients of manufactured hot dogs. These dogs make a quick and easy weeknight dinner. Simply combine the ingredients, form into hot dogs and put in the oven for 35 minutes. It makes enough for dinner, and for lunch for the next day!

Quick Tip: If you'd like to use ground turkey or chicken, that works too.

Prep: 20 minutes ✿ *Bake:* 40 minutes ✿ *Oven:* 350°F ✿ *Makes:* 6 servings

---

2 eggs

½ cup minced yellow onion

½ cup blanched almond flour

¼ cup flax meal

2 Tbsp. canned coconut milk, full fat

1 tsp. Dijon mustard

¼ tsp. black pepper

12 oz. cooked ham slices

12 oz. ground pork

1 avocado, peeled

1 red bell pepper

¼ cup chopped fresh cilantro

2 tomatoes

½ cup pico de gallo

Cilantro Dressing (page 162)

Fluffy Egg White Biscuits (page 154), shaped into hot dog buns

---

1) Preheat the oven to 350°F. Lightly grease a baking pan with coconut oil.

2) In a medium bowl, beat the eggs. Add the almond flour, flax meal, coconut milk, Dijon, and black pepper.

3) Pulse the ham in a food processor until finely ground.

4) Add the ground ham and ground pork to the bowl. Mix well. Don't be afraid to use your hands! Form into hot dogs. Place on the prepared baking pan. Bake for 40 minutes, until cooked through.

5) Arrange the cooked hot dogs on Fluffy Egg White Biscuits, shaped into buns. Top with the fresh, chopped produce and drizzle with Cilantro Dressing. Enjoy!

BEEF BRISKET

This is one of our favorite dinners. And it's easy to see why. Tender, fall-apart slices of brisket make a mouth-watering meal. Add a simple, dark green salad, a baked sweet potato, and a Fluffy Egg White Biscuit, and you've got a great meal. Oh and maybe a glass of red wine . . .

Quick Tip: In addition to being one of the most delicious dishes I've ever made, this also ranks as one of the easiest. Don't let the lengthy cook time deter you. It's as as simple as mixing up a marinade, letting it sit over-night, and then popping it in the oven to slow cook for half of the day. Make it on the weekend and enjoy the delightful aroma as you putter around the house waiting for dinnertime.

Prep: 10 minutes ❁ *Cook:* 4 hours ❁ *Oven:* 300°F ❁ *Makes:* 12 servings

1 lemon
5 garlic cloves
4 cups beef broth
1 cup coconut aminos
1 Tbsp. liquid smoke
5 lb. beef brisket

1) Combine all of the ingredients, except the brisket, in a bowl. Mix well.

2) Place the brisket in a large roasting pan, fat side up. Cover with the marinade. Cover the roasting pan tightly with foil. Marinate in the fridge for 24–48 hours. Let those juices do their flavorful magic!

3) Roast at 300°F for 4 hours, or 40 minutes per pound. Remove the foil after 4 hours, place under the high broil for a few minutes to lightly char the top. Transfer to a cutting board and slice. Put the slices back in the juices. Serve hot. Enjoy!

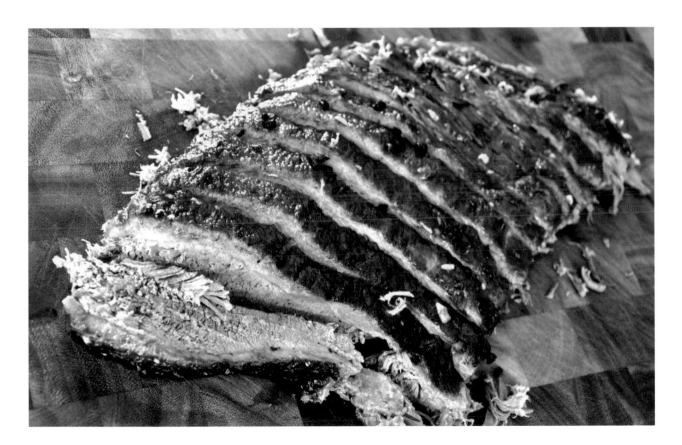

SIMPLE SPAGHETTI

What's a comfort food cookbook without a hold-me recipe for simple spaghetti? This is one of my favorite noodle dishes. It looks so similar to traditional spaghetti at first glance, yet it's worlds apart upon closer examination. Traditional spaghetti dinners are made with calorie-dense, gluten-filled noodles, topped with from-a-jar marinara sauce and sprinkled with cheese. This spaghetti dinner is made with zucchini noodles, a simple sauce from fresh tomatoes, and sprinkled with a nut-and-nutritional yeast topping. It's guilt free.

The guilt-free factor may be what first prompts you to attempt this recipe, but the taste is what's going to draw you back to it time and time again.

Quick Tip: For the first time in 100 years, our children's life expectancies are declining due to the increase in obesity. How will you make a difference with the kids in your life?

Prep: 15 minutes ✿ *Cook:* 40 minutes ✿ *Makes:* 4 servings

4 tomatoes

1 yellow onion

2 garlic cloves

¼ cup chopped fresh basil

2 Tbsp. olive oil

¼ tsp. sea salt

1 Tbsp. coconut palm sugar

4 zucchini, turned into noodles

¼ cup "Cheese" Sprinkle (page 164)

1) Heat the olive oil in a large skillet. Add the onion, garlic, and basil. Sauté until the onion is tender, about 5 minutes. Add the sea salt and coconut palm sugar.

2) Heat to a boil. Reduce and simmer, uncovered, for 40 minutes, or until the sauce has thickened. Serve over zucchini noodles with a spoonful of "Cheese" Sprinkle. Enjoy!

CREAMY CHICKEN NOODLES

Let's have a heart-to-heart . . . about noodles.

A big plate of warm noodles topped with creamy sauce is a classic comfort food. There's the nostalgia of family dinners past coupled with the naughty, feel-good effect that accompanies a mouthful of starchy carbs. But let's be honest, eating noodles—as comforting as it may be—is not something that we are able to do with a clear conscience.

As much as I'd love to serve noodle-filled dinners to my family, these dinners could put us on the fast track to obesity and health issues. But I wasn't ready to give up on noodles just yet; there had to be a way to create healthy, delicious noodle dishes that would not only taste good and deliver comfort, but would be grain-free, fiber-filled, and easy to make.

This creamy, comforting dish is 100 percent grain-, gluten- and dairy-free, which you'll find hard to believe when you dig into it. Remember to come up for air as you enjoy this tasty noodle dinner with zero guilt!

Quick Tip: Wondering what nutritional yeast is? Well, for starters, it's nothing like the fast action yeast that is used to make bread. It has large, yellow flakes and a nutty, cheesy flavor. It is fortified with B12 and sold in the bulk section of your local health food store. I add it to recipes to amp up the cheesy flavor, like with the creamy sauce in this recipe.

Prep: 30 minutes ❀ *Cook:* 30 minutes ❀ *Makes:* 6 servings

---

2 chicken breasts, cut into 1-inch cubes

¾ tsp. garlic powder, divided

1 tsp. sea salt, divided

½ tsp. onion powder, divided

½ tsp. black pepper, divided

¼ tsp. sweet paprika

½ tsp. dried basil

½ tsp. dried oregano

¼ tsp. dried thyme

1 lemon

1 Tbsp. olive oil

1 yellow onion

2 heads broccoli

2 cups mushrooms

1 Tbsp. coconut oil

1 Tbsp. coconut flour

1 (13.66-oz.) can coconut milk, full fat

½ cup nutritional yeast

1 Tbsp. Dijon mustard

1 Tbsp. mirin or white wine

zucchini noodles

---

1) Rinse the chicken breast and pat dry. Cut into 1-inch cubes. Gather the first amount of garlic powder, sea salt, onion powder, black pepper, and the sweet paprika, dried basil, dried oregano, dried thyme, and lemon. Juice and zest the lemon. Combine in a bowl and mix until the chicken pieces are evenly coated.

2) Heat the olive oil in a skillet over medium high heat. Add the chicken and cook for about 10 minutes, until there is no longer any pink in the chicken.

3) Wash the broccoli and wipe the mushrooms. Chop the onions and broccoli. Slice the mushrooms. Place in a skillet with an inch of water. Bring to a boil for 5 minutes. Drain and set the cooked veggies aside.

4) In a large skillet, melt the coconut oil over medium heat. Whisk in the coconut flour and continue to whisk until browned. Add the coconut milk, nutritional yeast, Dijon, mirin, garlic powder, onion powder, sea salt, and black pepper. Whisk frequently until the sauce begins to boil. Reduce the heat to a simmer and continue whisking for 5 minutes, as the sauce thickens.

5) Add the chicken to the sauce. Mix well. Arrange each plate with a pile of flat zucchini noodles, a spoonful of veggies, and a heaping scoop of the creamy chicken. Enjoy!

BEEF NOODLE BOWL

Some days you just need to eat a giant bowl of noodles. Add some savory beef and veggies and you're in heaven. While traditional beef noodle bowls will leave you bloated with a tummy ache, this noodle bowl will leave you lean and happy. It's all in the noodles. These ones are really zucchini in disguise. Shhhh, don't tell anyone. Just offer them a delicious bowl and smile slyly to yourself.

Quick Tip: I buy thinly sliced rib eye from my local Asian market. It comes both fresh and frozen, and it saves me the time and headache of trying to thinly slice the beef myself. If you are unable to locate rib eye that's been presliced, then freeze a piece of rib eye and use a mandoline slicer to perfectly and quickly slice it.

Prep: 15 minutes ✿ *Cook:* 15 minutes ✿ *Makes:* 4 servings

½ cup sake

½ cup mirin

½ cup coconut aminos

2 Tbsp. pure maple syrup

2 Tbsp. minced fresh ginger

2 Tbsp. minced fresh garlic

1 lb. rib eye, thinly sliced

1 head broccoli

3 carrots

2 tsp. toasted sesame oil

5 zucchini

1) Combine the sake, mirin, coconut aminos, syrup, ginger, and garlic in a bowl. Mix well. Arrange the sliced rib eye in a shallow pan. Pour half of the marinade over the beef. Save the remaining marinade in a bowl in the fridge.

2) Bring a large pot of water to boil. Chop the broccoli into florets and slice the carrots. Add the veggies to the boiling water for 5 minutes. Drain the veggies. Place in a large serving bowl.

3) Place a large skillet over medium-high heat. Add the sesame oil. Add the marinated rib eye and cook, stirring often. Cook the rib eye until all the pink is gone. Drain the skillet and add the cooked meat to the bowl of cooked veggies.

4) Peel the zucchini. Run the peeled zucchini through a spiral slicer to create long, thin noodles. Add the noodles to the bowl of meat and veggies. Pour the reserved marinade to the bowl and mix well. Serve immediately and enjoy!

CRISPY CHICKEN

Fried chicken is the ultimate comfort food. But greasy, lardy chicken pieces are not healthy, so I came up with this baked version. This recipe takes fried chicken to a happy, healthy place.

Quick Tip: It's important to get the hang of broiling when mastering the art of faux fried foods. On most ovens there is a button to switch the oven into high broil mode, which switches the heat source solely to the top. Move an oven rack close to the top and place your tray on it. Watch very closely as the food begins to crisp and brown, and then remove the tray quickly if the food begins to char.

Prep: 20 minutes ❁ *Bake:* 35 minutes ❁ *Oven:* 350°F ❁ *Makes:* 6 servings

2 eggs

2 Tbsp. fruit-only apricot preserves

2 Tbsp. Dijon mustard

½ tsp. garlic powder

½ tsp. sweet paprika

½ cup blanched almond flour

½ cup almond meal

½ cup coconut flour

¼ tsp. black pepper

¼ tsp. red pepper

½ tsp. sea salt

2 lb. boneless, skinless chicken tenders

1) Preheat the oven to 350°F. Lightly grease a 9 × 13 baking pan with coconut oil.

2) In a shallow bowl, combine the eggs, apricot preserves, Dijon, garlic powder, and sweet paprika.

3) In another shallow bowl, combine the almond flour, almond meal, coconut flour, black pepper, red pepper, and sea salt. Take 1 tablespoon of the dry ingredient mixture and add it to the wet ingredient mixture. Mix well.

4) Rinse the chicken tenders and pat dry. Arrange the bowls next to the chicken, with the prepared pan within reach. Dip the chicken in the egg mixture. Dredge through the flour mixture. Place the coated chicken pieces on the prepared pan.

5) Bake for 35 minutes. Turn the oven to high broil for 2 minutes, or until crispy. Serve with a side of Lazy Man's Ranch (page 160). Enjoy!

CRISPY ORANGE CHICKEN

This recipe is my answer to Chinese takeout. It's crispy, sweet, and oh-so-satisfying. If you've tried the awesome crispy orange chicken recipe on my blog, RealHealthyRecipes.com, then you'll notice that this new version has one major improvement: the chicken is battered. This version is crispier, tastier, and so much like takeout that you'll forget that it's grain- and soy-free.

Quick Tip: While battering the chicken makes it taste better, it does take a bit more time. When you're in a jam and need orange chicken ASAP, make this recipe without battering the chicken.

Prep: 25 minutes ✿ *Cook:* 25 minutes ✿ *Makes:* 6 servings

---

1 egg

½ cup chicken broth

½ cup arrowroot starch

3 Tbsp. coconut flour

½ cup frozen orange juice concentrate, no sugar added

3 Tbsp. coconut aminos

1 Tbsp. olive oil

1 orange

3 garlic cloves, minced

½ tsp. stevia powder

2 lb. boneless, skinless chicken thighs, cut into bite-size pieces

1 Tbsp. coconut oil

dash of sea salt and black pepper

dash of onion powder

2 green onions

1 Tbsp. sesame seeds

---

1) Combine the egg, chicken broth, arrowroot starch, and coconut flour in a bowl to form a batter. Mix well.

2) Combine the orange juice concentrate, coconut aminos, olive oil, orange zest, garlic cloves, and stevia.

3) Rinse the chicken and pat dry. Trim the fat and cut into bite sized pieces. Gather the coconut oil and a dash of sea salt, black pepper, and onion powder. Toss the chicken pieces with the spices. Mix the chicken pieces into the batter until evenly coated.

4) Place the coconut oil in a large skillet over medium high heat. Add the battered chicken pieces. Cook until evenly golden. Add the orange mixture to the skillet. Bring to a simmer and continue to cook as the sauce thickens, about 8 minutes. Remove from heat.

5) Chop the green onions. Sprinkle each serving with a tablespoon of green onions and a pinch of sesame seeds. Enjoy!

ONE POT CHICKEN DINNER WITH WHITE WINE AND GARLIC

I love simple dinner recipes that taste amazing and don't dirty many dishes. This recipe is a combination of three things that I love: chicken, white wine, and garlic.

Quick Tip: Real healthy dinners don't have to be fancy or complicated. Simple, wholesome ingredients like chicken and vegetables are the cornerstone of a well rounded diet.

Prep: 15 minutes ✻ *Cook:* 50 minutes ✻ *Makes:* 8 servings

⅓ cup coconut flour

sea salt and black pepper

3 lb. boneless, skinless chicken thighs

2 yellow onions, cut into half moon slices

2 heads garlic

2 Tbsp. olive oil

1 cup sparkling white wine

1 cup chicken broth

---

1) Combine the coconut flour and a pinch of salt and pepper in a small bowl. Mix well. Rinse the chicken and pat dry. Arrange the chicken next to the bowl of flour and a clean plate.

2) Coat the chicken pieces with the flour mixture and place on the clean plate. Brown both sides of each chicken piece. If your pot isn't big enough to fit all the pieces on the bottom, do this in batches. Once the chicken pieces are browned, remove from the pot and set aside on a clean plate.

3) Add the onion and garlic to the pot. Reduce the heat to medium. Cook until the onions soften. Add the broth, wine and chicken to the pot.

4) Cover and simmer for about 20 minutes, until the chicken is cooked through. Plate the chicken and spoon garlic, onion, and sauce on each piece. Enjoy!

OSSO BUCO

My husband, B, spent his early years in a tiny little village in Armenia where lamb was often the main course. Tender, braised, falling-off-the-bone lamb is his favorite meal. The idea of cooking lamb—a meat that I didn't even taste until adulthood—was pretty darn intimidating. Until this recipe. It's so easy! Really, I promise—cross my heart and hope to die—you can make this recipe. And everyone will swoon and liken you to a five-star chef. Promise.

Quick Tip: You've got some leeway with the cook time of this recipe. Sometimes I'll leave it in the oven for 3 hours instead of 2. You want the meat to be really tender and to fall off the bone. When in doubt, leave it in for 20 more minutes. The house smells so amazing while it cooks!

Prep: 15 minutes ❁ *Bake*: 2–2½ hours ❁ *Oven*: 350°F ❁ *Makes*: 6 servings

---

2 sweet potatoes

5 large carrots

1 yellow onion

1 (15-oz.) can San Marzano tomatoes

5 garlic cloves, chopped

2 Tbsp. olive oil

1 (750-ml.) bottle white wine

large pinch sea salt

large pinch black pepper

4 lamb shanks, cross-cut

---

1) Preheat the oven to 350°F.

2) Peel and roughly chop the veggies. Place the veggies in a heavy duty cooking pot with a tight fitting lid. Place the lamb shanks on top of the veggies. Top with the tomatoes, garlic, wine, salt and pepper.

3) Cover the pot with a lid and placc in the preheated oven for 2–2½ hours. You'll know the lamb is ready when it falls off the bone. Serve warm and enjoy!

SUZY'S BAKED CATFISH

My mother-in-law, Suzy, is seriously the cutest lady you'll ever meet. From the moment you step into her cozy kitchen you feel at home. Yummy smells fill your nose, a mechanical lobster mounted on the wall belts out a tune, and a heaping plate of warm food finds its way into your hands. Though we come from very different backgrounds—she grew up in Armenia and Syria in the '40s and speaks Armenian, while I'm a product of the '80s, grew up in northern Washington state, and speak English—we have a common love for cooking.

We both cook by feeling, using our instincts over cookbooks.

Suzy watches Turkish cooking shows, takes notes in Armenian, and then shares the recipes with me in our shared Armen-glish. When Suzy makes this recipe she doubles or even triples it, and then serves it family-style alongside platters of rice pilaf, cabbage salad, Armenian cheese, garden fresh veggies, and whole wheat lavash.

Quick Tip: Simple, fresh ingredients always make the most delicious meals. That's something that I've learned from Suzy, who grows most of her own vegetables and herbs in the backyard.

Prep: 15 minutes ❁ *Bake:* 35 minutes ❁ *Oven:* 350°F ❁ *Makes:* 4 servings

---

1 bunch fresh cilantro

1 tsp. olive oil

1 lemon

4 garlic cloves, finely minced

3 Tbsp. curry powder

3 Tbsp. sea salt

3 Tbsp. sweet paprika

4 catfish fillets

---

1) Preheat the oven to 350°F. Grease a baking pan with the olive oil. Gather and wash the cilantro. Trim the ends. Scatter the cilantro over the bottom of the baking pan.

2) Juice the lemon, saving 4 thin slices, and mince the garlic. Combine the lemon and garlic in a small bowl. Gather small bowls of curry powder, sweet paprika, and sea salt.

3) Rinse the fillets and pat dry. Generously rub the fillets with the spices. Arrange the fillets in the prepared pan. Drizzle each fillet with the lemon and garlic mixture. Top with sliced lemons.

4) Cover the pan with foil. Bake for 30 minutes. Remove the foil and bake for an additional 10 minutes. Serve with Mint Cabbage Salad (page 134).

TERIYAKI SALMON

Being from Washington state, I love salmon. Fresh, wild caught salmon marinated in teriyaki and grilled over an open flame is one of the sweet gifts of summer. This marinade tastes just like teriyaki, without the use of soy. When in doubt, add more garlic and ginger. You can never go wrong with more garlic and ginger.

Quick Tip: Saying no to junk food won't make you the most popular. In fact, it's going to make some of your friends and family uncomfortable and they may even give you a hard time about it. Don't be discouraged. Smile, laugh it off, and don't be pressured into eating something that isn't in line with your nutritional values.

Prep: 10 minutes ⚙ *Bake:* 20 minutes ⚙ *Oven:* 350°F ⚙ *Makes:* 2 servings

---

3 Tbsp. minced garlic

3 Tbsp. minced ginger

1 cup coconut aminos

¼ cup raw honey

2 salmon fillets

2 Tbsp. sesame seeds

2 green onions, thinly sliced

---

1) Preheat the oven to 350°F. Line a baking sheet with parchment paper.

2) Peel and finely mince the garlic and ginger. Combine with the coconut aminos and honey in a bowl.

3) Rinse the fillets and pat dry. Combine the fillets with the marinade in a large ziploc bag. Chill in the fridge for 40 minutes.

4) Arrange the fillets in a baking dish. Bake for 20 minutes. Turn the broiler on high for a couple of minutes to brown the tops. Serve on Cauliflower Rice (page 122) and top with sesame seeds and sliced green onions. Enjoy!

BEEF STEW

Okra is one of my all-time favorite comfort foods. There's something delicious about biting into the tender okra skin and then having the seeds pop in your mouth. This stew is incredibly simple and easy to make in the slow cooker.

Quick Tip: This stew is much, much tastier with fresh okra. But fresh okra can be tricky to find, depending on where you live. Canned or frozen okra can be subbed if fresh is not available.

Prep: 15 minutes ❁ *Cook:* 6 hours ❁ *Makes:* 6 servings

---

1 lb. beef stew meat, cut into 1-inch cubes

1 Tbsp. olive oil

dash of sea salt and black pepper

4 cloves garlic, minced

1 cup baby carrots, sliced lengthwise and crosswise

1 large yellow onion, chopped

1 lb. fresh or canned okra

3 tomatoes, chopped

1 cup chicken broth

½ tsp. dried oregano

½ tsp. ground cumin

1 tsp. dried thyme

⅛ tsp. ground allspice

2 Tbsp. tomato paste

---

1) In a skillet over medium-high heat, combine the beef, olive oil, sea salt, and pepper. Sear the meat then remove from heat.

2) Combine all of the ingredients in a slow cooker. Mix well. Cover and cook on high for 6 hours. Enjoy!

SIDES

. . . . for that perfect meal

CAULIFLOWER RICE

If you haven't yet been introduced to the concept of cauliflower rice, allow me to do the introduction. Cauliflower rice, meet my dear, recipe-loving friend. Dear friend, meet cauliflower rice.

Cauliflower rice is shredded cauliflower that is seasoned, lightly cooked, and served as you would traditional grain rice. It's low in calories, low in carbs, and high in awesomeness.

Quick Tip: There are soooo many ways that you can make cauliflower rice. This is the most basic version. In the following pages you'll find recipes for island-style fried rice, wild rice, and shiitake stir-fried rice. Yum, yum, and yum!

Prep: 10 minutes ✺ *Cook:* 5 minutes ✺ *Makes:* 4 servings

1 head cauliflower
1 Tbsp. olive oil
sea salt
black pepper

1) Wash the cauliflower and discard the leaves. Chop into small florets. Run the florets through the food processor with a grating attachment to create small, rice-like pieces.

2) Pour the olive oil into a large skillet over medium heat. Add the shredded cauliflower to the skillet. Sauté for 5 minutes or until tender, and then season with salt and pepper. Enjoy as a side to your favorite entrée!

SHIITAKE STIR-FRIED RICE

Most of my recipes are inspired by traditional recipes that I think can be made healthier. Like this recipe for shiitake stir fried rice. I saw a stunning photo of a fried rice recipe using these veggies that made my mouth water. Then I remembered how heavy and bloated I feel after eating traditional fried rice. Sure, it tastes really good, but the overload of grain wouldn't be worth the dip in energy and subsequent weight gain.

Rather than eat a plate of steamed veggies when I'm craving fried rice, I came up with this recipe that has the look, feel, and flavor of traditional stir-fried rice.

Try it for yourself! Your taste buds won't believe that you're simply eating vegetables and egg.

Quick Tip: How amazing will you feel when you reach your goal weight? How elated will you be when your doctor tells you that your health has improved? How exciting will it be when your significant other notices how extra attractive you're getting? How satisfying will it be when your coworkers, friends, and family ask you what you're doing differently to look so energetic and lean? How confident will you feel when you look in the mirror and not only love what you see but also feel a sense of pride and accomplishment for the responsible, health-conscious person that you've become? Keep going, one bite of cauliflower rice at a time. You've got this!

Prep: 15 minutes ❁ *Cook:* 15 minutes ❁ *Makes:* 6 servings

2 eggs

2 Tbsp. olive oil, divided

1 yellow onion

2 carrots

1 red bell pepper

1 cup shiitake mushrooms

2 tsp. fresh ginger, peeled and minced

2 garlic cloves, minced

½ cup snow peas

3 Tbsp. coconut aminos

2 Tbsp. apple cider vinegar

1 head cauliflower, shredded

1) Beat the eggs in a bowl. Heat 1 tablespoon olive oil in a large skillet. Add the beaten eggs, and swirl them to coat the bottom of the pan. Don't stir. Cook for 2 minutes until set. Transfer the egg to a cutting board and slice into strips.

2) Chop the onion. Thinly slice the carrots into matchsticks. Seed and thinly slice the bell pepper. Remove the mushroom stems and slice. Remove the stems and strings from the snow peas and slice diagonally.

3) Heat the remaining 1 tablespoon olive oil in a large skillet. Add the onions and cook until soft. Add the carrots and red peppers to the skillet. Add the mushrooms to the skillet. Add the ginger, garlic, and snow peas to the skillet. Add the shredded cauliflower to the skillet. Add the coconut aminos and vinegar. Stir often and cook for 5 minutes. Fold in the sliced egg. Enjoy!

ISLAND-STYLE FRIED RICE

There's a little restaurant in Maui called The Gazebo, on the south side of Napili bay. It's small and eclectic, tucked to the side of a motel's small pool deck and nearly touching the sprawling Pacific Ocean. On our last visit we waited outside, in the rain, for over an hour to get a table. And we didn't even complain once, because we knew what was in store for us. The Gazebo is known for 2 things: their phenomenal macadamia nut pancakes and their island-style fried rice. While I can justify eating a breakfast like that while on vacation, I simply had to come up with a healthy version to make at home on the regular. It turned out ahhhmazing. Stand-in-the-rain worthy.

Quick Tip: Starting today, eat in a way that your future self will thank you for. Words to live by, my friend, words to live by.

Prep: 15 minutes ❀ *Cook:* 15 minutes ❀ *Makes:* 6 servings

---

12 oz. sliced ham

2 chicken sausage links

1 cup fresh pineapple

3 green onions

3 eggs

1 Tbsp. olive oil

1 head cauliflower, shredded

3 Tbsp. coconut aminos

1 tsp. garlic powder

---

1) Chop the ham and sausage into small pieces. Peel and chop the pineapple. Thinly slice the green onion.

2) Whisk the eggs in a bowl.

3) Place the meat in a skillet with olive oil. Cook until browned, stirring often. Remove the meat from the skillet.

4) Pour the egg mixture into the hot skillet. Scramble the eggs and set aside.

5) Add the shredded cauliflower to the hot skillet. Stir in the meat, pineapple, egg, coconut aminos, and garlic powder. Mix and cook for 10 minutes, until tender. Top with sliced green onion. Enjoy!

WILD RICE

Before going grain-free, wild rice used to be one of my favorite side dishes. The flavor and consistency of wild rice went perfectly with a tender serving of protein. My grain-free plate felt empty. A few months after creating my first cauliflower rice recipe, I had the epiphany to come up with a version of cauliflower rice with the look, feel, and taste of wild rice. This recipe calls for shredded cauliflower, brussels sprouts, chopped dates, and chopped walnuts. The end result is amazingly similar to traditional wild rice.

Quick Tip: This recipe for wild rice is my go-to accompaniment for holiday meals. It pairs wonderfully with turkey and ham.

Prep: 15 minutes ✿ *Bake:* 35 minutes ✿ *Oven:* 400°F ✿ *Makes:* 8 servings

1 onion, chopped
1 Tbsp. olive oil
1 cup brussels sprouts
4 celery stalks
½ cup pitted and chopped dates
½ cup shelled and chopped walnuts
1 cup chicken broth
pinch of sea salt and black pepper
1 head cauliflower, shredded
¼ cup chopped pistachio (for garnish)

1) Preheat the oven to 400°F. Lightly grease a casserole dish with olive oil.

2) Place the olive oil in a skillet over medium high heat. Add the chopped onion. Cook the onion until soft, about 10 minutes. Remove from heat.

3) Run the brussels sprouts and celery through a food processor with the grating attachment. Add the shredded brussels sprouts, celery, and cauliflower to the skillet. Return to heat. Add the chicken broth and a pinch of sea salt and pepper. Cook for 3 minutes.

4) Transfer the rice mixture to the prepared pan. Cover with foil and bake for 35 minutes. Stir in the dates and walnuts. Return to the oven, uncovered, for 10 minutes. Garnish with chopped pistachios. Enjoy!

TABBOULEH

Tabbouleh is a beloved side dish in B's family. The recipe originated in Syria and was then spread to Armenia and other neighboring countries. Traditionally the salad is made with bulgur, a cereal made from durum wheat. However it's the other ingredients that give Tabbouleh its amazing flavor.

Tomatoes, cucumbers, finely chopped parsley, mint, onion, garlic, olive oil, lemon juice, and salt are the true heart of this flavorful dish. In recent years, tabbouleh has become a popular dish in the United States. You've probably seen it at the salad bar in Whole Foods or served in your local deli.

I absolutely love the flavors of this classic salad, but the bulgur was a problem. Too many carbs and too many calories. So I decided to try shredded jicama in place of the bulgur. This removed the gluten and grains from the dish, making it lighter, lower in carbs, and more refreshing. This Tabbouleh is truly delicious! You get to enjoy all of the flavors of classic tabbouleh without the repercussions of the bulgur.

Quick Tip: I like the fresh, sweet flavor of jicama for this salad but if you prefer cauliflower, that is another option. Shred the cauliflower as you would the jicama and mix it in raw with the other ingredients.

Prep: 15 minutes ❂ *Makes:* 12 servings

---

1 bunch green onions

½ cup fresh mint leaves

1 cup flat leaf parsley

1 cucumber

2 cups cherry tomatoes

1 jicama

½ tsp. sea salt

dash black pepper

juice from ½ lemon

2 Tbsp. olive oil

2 cloves garlic, minced

---

1) Peel the jicama and cut into 1-inch pieces. Run the pieces through a food processor with the grating attachment so that it is finely shredded. Place the shredded jicama in a large bowl.

2) Finely chop the green onions, mint, parsley, cucumber, and cherry tomatoes. Add to the bowl.

3) In a small bowl, combine the lemon juice, olive oil, sea salt, pepper, and garlic. Mix well, and then pour over the salad. Toss. Taste and add more salt and pepper if needed. Serve chilled. Enjoy!

MINT CABBAGE SALAD

Here's another one of my mother-in-law, Suzy's, recipes. The simple, bold flavors of mint, garlic, and lemon make this cabbage salad something special. My favorite part of making this salad is the taste testing. At any family gathering you'll find the ladies in the kitchen, gathered around a huge bowl of cabbage salad. Add some more lemon. Okay, now how does it taste? More garlic. How about now? Another sprinkle of mint. Yum . . . perfection!

Quick Tip: Suzy dries her own mint from the garden each summer and stores the dried leaves in a big jar. To dry fresh mint, wash in cold water and pat dry. Arrange the leaves in a single layer on a baking sheet and place in an open oven at 180°F for 2–4 hours.

Prep: 5 minutes ✸ *Makes:* 6 servings

1 head green cabbage

2 Tbsp. dried mint

juice from 1 lemon

4 garlic cloves, minced

1 tsp. olive oil

pinch of sea salt

1) Wash the cabbage and discard the outer leaves. Slice the cabbage very thinly and place in a large bowl.

2) Combine the mint, lemon, garlic, and olive oil in a small bowl. Mix well.

3) Pour the mint dressing over the sliced cabbage. Add sea salt to taste. Enjoy!

PASTA SALAD

What picnic would be complete without a cold, olive-dotted bowl of pasta salad? Gee, traditional pasta salad doesn't even sound appetizing to me anymore. I can anticipate how all those refined, gluten-filled carbs would feel in my tummy, and how sluggish and zapped I'd feel afterwards. So I set out to create a pasta salad without guilt, without gluten, and without a sluggish aftereffect.

The solution was simple: noodles, simply made with a vegetable peeler and zucchini, create the perfect base for pasta salad flavors. Serve this salad up alongside a grilled steak for an amazing, wholesome dinner that's big on flavor.

Quick Tip: Here are three ways to create low-carb noodles out of squash:

1. Use spaghetti squash. This is the least labor-intensive of the three methods since the noodle strands are naturally part of the spaghetti squash. Wash the spaghetti squash, poke it all over with a fork, and bake at 375°F for an hour. Cool and then slice in half. Scoop out and discard the seeds and pulp, then scrape the long squash noodles out.

2. Use a simple vegetable peeler. In this recipe, and also in the recipe for Creamy Chicken Noodles (page 102), I simply use a standard vegetable peeler to create long, flat noodles. It's easy, quick, and cost effective.

3. Use a spiral slicer. Spiral slicers are really cool because it makes the zucchini noodles really look like traditional noodles. You can also vary the size and width of the noodles, taking it from angel hair-size to spaghetti noodle-size.

Prep: 20 minutes ❁ *Makes:* 4 servings

3 zucchini
½ cup cherry tomatoes, sliced in half
¼ cup sliced black olives
2 Tbsp. olive oil
1 garlic clove, minced
juice of ½ lemon
1 tsp. dried basil
dash sea salt and black pepper

1) Gather and wash the zucchini. Trim the ends. Use a vegetable peeler to create long, flat noodles. Place the zucchini noodles in a large bowl.

2) Slice the olives and cherry tomatoes.

3) Combine the olive oil, garlic, lemon, dried basil, and a pinch of sea salt and black pepper in a small bowl.

4) Pour the dressing over the noodles. Add the tomatoes and olives. Mix well. Chill and serve cold. Enjoy!

CHILE PESTO NOODLES

Most of the time pesto is made with fresh basil leaves, olive oil, garlic, pine nuts, parmesan cheese, and a dash of sea salt, but today we are making pesto with some very interesting ingredients. Charred jalapeños, cilantro, and arugula are a fiery combination that completely wake up the taste buds!

While you may be tempted to purchase store-bought pesto, it's really worth the minimal effort needed to make your own. Not only does homemade pesto taste SO MUCH better, you're also able to make it dairy-free by leaving out the parmesan and preservatives. And let's be perfectly honest . . . throwing ingredients into a food processor is not what you'd call strenuous work. It's pretty darn easy.

Quick Tip: For a classic basil pesto try this simple dairy-free recipe: ½ cup raw walnuts, 3 cups fresh basil leaves, 4 garlic cloves, 1 teaspoon sea salt, ¼ cup olive oil, ½ cup nutritional yeast and 1 tablespoon lemon juice. Combine in a food processor.

Prep: 20 minutes ❁ *Cook:* 10 minutes ❁ *Makes:* 4 servings

3 green jalapeños

½ cup shelled pistachios

2 cups fresh cilantro

2 cups fresh arugula

1 Tbsp. fresh oregano

3 cloves garlic

1 Tbsp. ground cumin

juice from 1 lime

1/3 cup chicken broth

¼ cup olive oil

dash of sea salt and black pepper

4 organic zucchini, turned into noodles

1) Place the jalapeños on a grill pan over medium heat. Cook until evenly charred. Once the jalapeños are charred, remove from heat and place in a paper bag. Fold the bag closed and leave for 10 minutes. When cool enough to handle, rub off the skins with a paper towel. Slice in half and seed.

2) Place the pistachios in a small, dry skillet. Cook over medium heat until lightly toasted.

3) Placc the jalapeños, pistachios, arugula, oregano, garlic, cumin, lime, chicken broth, olive oil, sea salt, and black pepper in a food processor. Pulse until creamy. Place the zucchini noodles in a large bowl and mix with the pesto. Enjoy!

WHIPPED SWEET POTATO

This dish could be served as a side to dinner or as dessert. It's delightfully sweet and creamy. You know that marshmallow-smothered sweet potato dish that aunt Mildred always brings to holiday dinners? This is the recipe to replace that one with. Kapeesh?

Quick Tip: Not to sound cheesy, but do you love your body? I'll admit that, as a woman, this is an issue that I've struggled with on and off for as long as I can remember. It's easy to fall into the trap of only seeing your imperfections. And as the mother of a young daughter, I so dearly want her to live her life in grateful acceptance of herself. Eating only real, wholesome foods has brought me to a place of peace about my body. Nope, it's still not "perfect" and never will be. But it's healthy, it's strong, and it's capable, and that's a beautiful thing.

Prep: 15 minutes ❀ *Bake:* 40 minutes ❀ *Oven:* 400°F ❀ *Makes:* 6 servings

3 sweet potatoes

2 Tbsp. coconut oil

sea salt and black pepper

1 (13.66-oz.) can coconut milk, full fat

2 Tbsp. raw honey

1 Tbsp. coconut oil

1 tsp. ground cinnamon

scant ¼ tsp. sea salt

chopped pecans (optional for garnish)

unsweetened shredded coconut (optional for garnish)

1) Preheat the oven to 400°F.

2) Gather the sweet potatoes. Wash and brush with melted coconut oil. Place in a baking pan. Sprinkle the sweet potatoes with sea salt and black pepper and poke all over with a fork. Bake for 30–40 minutes, until fork tender. Cool and peel. Place in a food processor and blend until smooth.

3) Combine the coconut milk, honey, and coconut oil in a medium saucepan. Mix and heat over low heat for 10 minutes. Add the mixture to the food processor and blend until fully incorporated. Add the cinnamon and sea salt. Blend. Pour into a serving bowl. Chill for 20 minutes before serving. Garnish with chopped pecans and unsweetened shredded coconut if desired. Enjoy!

ALMOND BREAD

Bread is a huge part of our food culture. Some form of bread is included in nearly all restaurant- and home-cooked meals. We grew up eating bread, and we give our kids bread. Bread is part of who we are.

So what do you do when you figure out that all that bread is causing weight gain? Throw out your breadbox and be done with it?

Well, that approach would work, but I'd rather adapt my bread recipes by using real food ingredients and leaving the grains out. This way there's still a slice of something warm and soft to be eaten with dinner, and I can still make french toast on the weekends.

Yes, you can still enjoy a slice of bread while avoiding grains and gluten. This moist bread is made with almond meal, which gives it a delicious nutty flavor.

Quick Tip: This recipe could be made with either blanched almond flour or almond meal. The difference? Blanched almond flour is made with blanched almonds with the skins removed. Almond meal is made with almonds that still have their skins on. As a result, almond meal is heartier, darker in color, and produces baked goods that are more dense. Baked goods made with blanched almond flour are lighter in color and more delicate in texture.

Prep: 10 minutes ✿ *Bake:* 45 minutes ✿ *Oven:* 300°F ✿ *Makes:* 1 loaf

---

2 Tbsp. raw honey

5 cups blanched almond flour

1 tsp. baking soda

½ tsp. sea salt

6 eggs

2 tsp. apple cider vinegar

---

1) Preheat the oven to 300 degrees. Grease a loaf pan with coconut oil.

2) Place the raw honey in a small pot and put in a small skillet filled with water over medium heat. Mix occasionally until the honey melts. Remove from heat and cool.

3) Combine the almond flour, baking soda, and sea salt in a medium bowl.

4) Crack eggs into a large bowl. Whisk. Add the apple cider vinegar. Mix in the melted honey. Add the dry ingredients to the wet ingredients. Mix until well combined.

5) Place the dough into the prepared loaf pan. Smooth the top. Bake for 45 minutes or until golden and baked through. Loosed the side of the loaf immediately after removing from the oven, and then cool completely before removing from the pan. Enjoy!

COCONUT FLOUR TORTILLAS

Since going grain-free, I have learned to love the crunch of a lettuce-wrapped burger, taco, enchilada, and bur-rito . . . but alas, how can one really lettuce wrap an almond butter and jam sandwich? Not happening. That is actually what drove me to come up with this coconut flour–based recipe for tortillas—my desire for an almond butter and jam sandwich. Luckily for you these Coconut Flour Tortillas are also amazing served up with tacos, enchiladas, burritos, and with just about any topping you can think of.

Quick Tip: To ensure that your Coconut Flour Tortillas stick together and are sturdy enough to handle, follow these 4 steps:

1. Blend the batter until smooth. And then blend a little more.

2. Let the blended batter sit for 15 minutes to let the flax work its binding magic.

3. Preheat your griddle or skillet to medium-high heat, and then reduce to medium-low heat when you start to cook. As you are cooking the tortillas, don't flip until they get golden brown. These aren't pancakes, so realize that browning is much better than undercooking.

4. As you cook the tortillas, stack them with little pieces of parchment paper in between. Let the stack sit out at room temperature for 30–40 minutes. For some reason this really helps make the tortillas sturdier. Not sure why, but it works!

Prep: 5 minutes ❀ *Cook:* 20 minutes ❀ *Makes:* 12 tortillas

---

6 eggs
1 (13.66-oz.) can coconut milk, full fat
¼ cup coconut flour
¼ cup flax meal
½ tsp. baking soda
½ tsp. sea salt

---

1) Preheat a large skillet or pancake griddle over medium-high heat. Lightly grease with coconut oil.

2) Combine the ingredients in a high-speed blender. Blend until smooth. Let the batter sit for 15 minutes, so the flax can work its binding magic.

3) Reduce the heat to medium-low. Pour ⅓ cup batter onto the preheated griddle in a large tortilla shape. Allow to cook until set, and then flip to brown the other side. Repeat with all of the batter. Enjoy!

JALAPEÑO SKILLET CORNBREAD

Why make cornbread without corn? Because corn is a grain that contains gluten. Because corn is high in carbs and low in nutrients. Because corn is hard to digest. Because corn is second only to soy as the most commonly genetically modified food.

So when you have a craving for a hunk of warm cornbread with your dinner, this recipe for Jalapeño Skillet Cornbread saves the day.

Quick Tip: You don't really have to make this in a skillet if you don't want. If you prefer your cornbread to be square shaped, use a greased 8 × 8 pan. Sprinkle the cooked jalapenos on the bottom of the pan, or mix them into the batter. This bread is delicious sans jalapeños if you prefer. Simply skip steps 2 and 3.

Prep: 20 minutes ❁ *Bake:* 20 minutes ❁ *Oven:* 425°F ❁ *Makes:* 6 servings

---

4 fresh jalapeños

1 Tbsp. olive oil

1 Tbsp. minced garlic

1½ cups blanched almond flour

⅓ cup arrowroot starch

⅓ cup coconut flour

½ tsp. baking soda

¼ tsp. sea salt

¼ tsp. turmeric

4 eggs

¾ cup canned coconut milk, full fat

2 tsp. apple cider vinegar

¼ cup coconut oil

3 Tbsp. raw honey

---

1) Preheat the oven to 425°F.

2) Gather and wash 4 fresh jalapeños. Put on some gloves, or this part can be painful. Slice the jalapeños in half and remove the seeds. Mince the jalapeños.

3) Place the oil, garlic, and jalapeños in a medium, oven-proof skillet. Cook over medium heat until the jalapeños become tender. Remove from heat.

4) Combine the almond flour, arrowroot starch, coconut flour, baking soda, salt, and turmeric in a medium bowl.

5) In another bowl, combine the eggs, coconut milk, apple cider vinegar, coconut oil, and raw honey. Add the wet ingredients to the dry ones. Mix until just combined, removing any lumps with the spoon as you mix.

6) Rub the sides of the skillet with olive oil. Pour the batter over the jalapeños and smooth out the top. Bake for 20 minutes or until golden on top. Let sit for 5 minutes then invert on a cutting board and slice into wedges. Enjoy!

Keuilian

HERB FLATBREAD

I'm really jazzed about this recipe for Herb Flatbread. It only takes around 20 minutes, start to finish, and it's the perfect addition to a wholesome, lean dinner. Also it reminds me of an Indian bread recipe from high school home ec—my only other memory from that class being the salmonella lecture I received for repeatedly eating raw cookie dough. Some things never change.

Quick Tip: While this bread is delicious with herbs, it can also be made plain. Just leave out the herbs and garlic powder. Then make an almond butter and jelly sandwich. Oh, that sounds good . . .

Prep: 10 minutes ❁ *Cook:* 10 minutes ❁ *Makes:* 4 servings

---

1 cup blanched almond flour

1 cup arrowroot starch

½ tsp. sea salt

1 tsp. garlic powder

1 Tbsp. fresh oregano, finely chopped

1 Tbsp. fresh parsley, finely chopped

1 Tbsp. fresh thyme, finely chopped

1 egg

3 Tbsp. coconut oil, plus more for cooking

¼ cup warm water

---

1) Combine the almond flour, arrowroot starch, coconut oil, sea salt, garlic powder, and fresh herbs in a large bowl. Add the egg and coconut oil. Mix well. Add the warm water and mix to form a sticky batter.

2) Heat 1 tablespoon coconut oil in a large skillet over medium-high heat. Pour the batter by ¼ cup scoops onto the prepared skillet. Cook until golden, flip, and cook the other side to golden. Serve immediately. Enjoy!

GARLIC TOAST

Who doesn't love Garlic Toast? It's garlicky and toasty all at the same time. B found a plate of these one day while I was out of the house, and made fast business of them. Then I received a text with a picture of the half demolished plate with the caption, "Hope you already got a picture of these." Ha! I learned long ago not to leave food around without taking a glamour shot first.

Quick Tip: Going gluten- and grain-free is quite overwhelming at first. It's hard not to focus on all of the things that you are giving up. Rather than focusing on the negatives of your new diet, zero in on all of the positives. Make a list of all the fresh, new, delicious, and exciting foods that you can enjoy. And then seek out grain-free versions of your old favorites . . . like Garlic Toast.

Prep: 25 minutes ✽ *Bake:* 20 minutes ✽ *Oven:* 350°F ✽ *Makes:* 13 servings

¾ cup coconut oil

3 eggs

6 Tbsp. water

3 cups blanched almond flour

½ cup + 2 Tbsp. coconut flour

6 Tbsp. arrowroot starch

1 tsp. baking soda

1 tsp. sea salt

1½ tsp. cream of tartar

½ cup palm shortening

2 Tbsp. chopped garlic

2 Tbsp. freeze dried chives

1) Preheat the oven to 350°F. Lightly grease a pie dish with coconut oil.

2) Combine the coconut oil, eggs, and water in a bowl. Mix well.

3) Combine the almond flour, coconut flour, arrowroot starch, baking soda, sea salt, and cream of tartar in another bowl. Add the dry ingredients to the wet ones and mix well to form dough. Shape the dough into a ball. Wrap in plastic and chill in the fridge for 20 minutes.

4) Cream the palm shortening together with the garlic and chives.

5) Roll the dough flat between two pieces of parchment paper to form a large rectangle. Carefully remove the top parchment paper. Spread half of the garlic and chive mixture over the dough. Roll the dough up and slide a thin string under the dough and cross over the top. Pull both sides of the string to cleanly cut a slice of dough. Repeat with the rest of the dough roll.

6) Place the rolls in the prepared pie dish. Bake for 20 minutes. Turn on the high broil and brown the tops for a couple of minutes at the end to get really crispy. Rub the remaining garlic and chive mixture over the tops of the toasts. Enjoy!

FLUFFY EGG WHITE BISCUITS

It only took me 3 years to perfect a gluten-free biscuit . . . .and here it is, folks! In all of my previous attempts the biscuits inevitably turned out like hard rocks, or hockey pucks. Not exactly what I was going for. As Andrew, my 8 year old, would say, no bueno! This recipe, on the other hand, uses beaten egg whites to create a fluffy, delicate biscuit that not only tastes amazing but is amazing for you. These are also really quick to whip together; or you could start just 30 minutes before dinner and have them hot on the table.

Quick Tip: We don't like to waste perfectly good ingredients. That's not classy. So take all 8 of the yolks from this recipe, flip to page 216 and whip up some custard while the biscuits bake.

Prep: 15 minutes ✹ *Bake:* 15 minutes ✹ *Oven:* 350°F ✹ *Makes:* 12 biscuits

---

2 cups blanched almond flour

1 cup flax meal

½ cup arrowroot starch

⅓ cup coconut flour

1 tsp. baking soda

8 egg whites (Save those egg yolks for Custard on page 216 or Key Lime Pie on page 184)

2 Tbsp. raw honey

½ cup coconut oil

1 egg, whisked

---

1) Preheat the oven to 350°F. Line a baking sheet with parchment paper.

2) Gather the blanched almond flour, flax meal, arrowroot starch, coconut flour, and baking soda. Combine the gathered dry ingredients in a bowl. Mix well. Add the honey and coconut oil and mix to combine.

3) Whip the egg whites until soft peaks form. Combine the dough with the whipped egg whites. Carefully fold together with a large spoon.

4) Use an ice cream scooper to place large spoonfuls of dough onto the prepared pan. Whisk the egg in a small bowl with a fork and brush over the tops of the biscuits. Bake for 15 minutes, or until the biscuits are golden top. Enjoy!

ROASTED EGGPLANT

I am obsessed with this recipe. It all started when, for the first time EVER, my garden successfully produced a crop of Japanese eggplants. I came up with this recipe to cover the eggplants in a garlic-lemon-olive oil mixture, and then roast it to tender, golden perfection. It turned out amazingly good!

Since then I've been making this tasty eggplant dish at least once a week. I'm probably going to turn purple soon . . .

Quick Tip: The key to making this recipe extra delicious is to roast it until it's really really tender and golden. When in doubt, leave it in to roast a little longer.

Prep: 25 minutes ✿ *Bake:* 40 minutes ✿ *Oven:* 400°F ✿ *Makes:* 4 servings

---

5 Japanese eggplants

sea salt

¼ cup olive oil

1 Tbsp. minced garlic

juice of 1 lemon

---

1) Preheat the oven to 400°F. Lightly grease a rimmed baking sheet with olive oil.

2) Slice the eggplants in half, lengthwise, and arrange in a single layer on the baking sheet. Sprinkle the cut side of each eggplant with sea salt Let sit for 20 minutes, until some liquid is drawn out. Wipe the liquid and salt off with a paper towel.

3) Combine the olive oil, garlic, and lemon juice in a small bowl. Rub the olive oil mixture over the tops of the eggplants. Roast for 30–40 minutes. Enjoy!

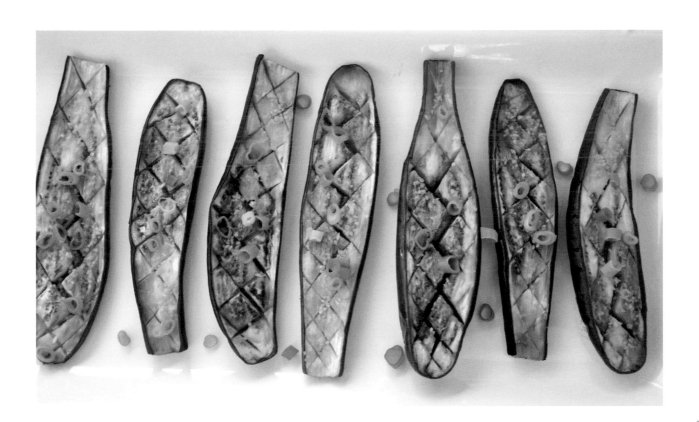

COLLARD GREENS

I can't explain my love of collard greens. I grew up in the Northwest, not the south, and I hadn't even tasted collards until well into adulthood. And yet, I'm hooked. Quite curious. This recipe is savory, satisfying, and addicting. There's something so comforting about tender, bacon-dotted greens. Mmmmmmmm.

Quick Tip: Collards need those thick, fibrous stems to be taken out and discarded before cooking. To quickly do so, fold the large leaf in half and use a knife to slice down through both layers of the green, along the length of the stem.

Prep: 10 minutes ❁ *Cook:* 2 hours ❁ *Makes:* 6 servings

---

3 slices bacon, chopped

1 large bunch collard greens, stemmed and chopped

1 large yellow onion, chopped

4 cups chicken broth

2 Tbsp. coconut palm sugar

2 garlic cloves, minced

1 tsp. sea salt

2 Tbsp. apple cider vinegar

½ tsp. ground red pepper

¼ tsp. black pepper

---

1) Place the bacon in a large skillet over medium heat. Cook until done but not crispy.

2) Add the collards and onion to the skillet. Cook until the greens wilt. Add the broth to the skillet and bring to a boil. Add the coconut palm sugar, garlic, sea salt, vinegar, red pepper, and black pepper.

3) Cover and cook over low heat for an hour. Uncover and continue to cook on low for another hour. Enjoy!

LAZY MAN'S RANCH

If my daughter, Chloe, had it her way, she'd put ranch dressing on everything. Chicken, veggies, hamburgers, fries, pizza, and even a little in her hair when she's feeling wild. Bottled, dairy-filled ranch dressing has many nutritional problems stemming from the long list of highly processed, chemical ingredients, which is why it's much tastier to make your own. This recipe is quick, easy, and a delicious addition to chicken, veggies, hamburgers, fries, pizza, and even your hair, but we will draw the line there.

Quick Tip: Don't skip step 1! This is vital to making a dressing that is creamy and not runny. I know, it is going to take a little longer, and this is called Lazy Man's Ranch after all, but trust that I wouldn't make you do it if it wasn't important.

Prep: overnight + 5 minutes ❀ *Makes:* 4 servings

---

2 cans (13.66-oz.) coconut milk, full fat

1 Tbsp. dried parsley, crushed (or 3 Tbsp. fresh parsley, minced)

2 tsp. dried dill (or 2 Tbsp. fresh dill, minced)

2 tsp. onion powder

1 tsp. garlic salt

pinch of sea salt

pinch of black pepper

½ tsp. apple cider vinegar

---

1) Chill the 2 cans of coconut milk in the fridge overnight—do not shake. Turn the cans of coconut milk upside down, and use a can opener to remove the bottom of the can. Pour the liquid out, and then scoop the creamy, white coconut cream into a bowl.

2) Combine all of the ingredients in a food processor. Pulse until smooth and well combined. Chill for 15 minutes. Enjoy!

CILANTRO DRESSING

This simple dressing is filled with the refreshing flavor of cilantro. It's wonderful drizzled over fresh greens or a yummy taco salad.

Quick Tip: Stop buying salad dressing from the store. Immediately, this minute. Store-bought dressing is filled with harmful and toxic ingredients, so let's avoid it. Here's the equation for a wholesome, homemade salad dressing: 3 parts high quality oil, 1 part lemon juice or vinegar, dash of sea salt and fresh black pepper, and a few tablespoons of fresh or dried herbs.

Prep: 5 minutes ✿ *Makes:* 1 cup

1 (13.66-oz.) can coconut milk, chilled overnight

1 cup fresh cilantro, trimmed and chopped

2 Tbsp. lime juice

1 clove garlic

½ cup olive oil

2 tsp. apple cider vinegar

½ tsp. sea salt

dash of black pepper

1) Chill the can of coconut milk in the fridge overnight. Do NOT shake the cans up at all! Ever! Carefully turn the cans over and open from the bottom. Drain out the liquid and scoop the white cream into a blender. Discard the liquid.

2) Add the remaining ingredients to the blender. Blend until smooth. Chill for 20 minutes. Enjoy!

"CHEESE" SPRINKLE

This cheese substitute has a nutty, cheesy flavor and is really easy to make. Sprinkle it on zucchini noodles, enchiladas, meatballs, steamed veggies, scrambled eggs, or anything that you would sprinkle cheese on.

Quick Tip: "Cheese" Sprinkle and Dairy-Free Cheese Spread (page 166) are best made in a big batch every 10 days and kept in an airtight container in the fridge. This way you have your cheese substitute on hand when you need it. Cuz you never know when you're going to get the urge for "Cheese" Sprinkles.

Prep: 10 minutes ❁ *Cook:* 10 minutes ❁ *Makes:* 2 cups

1 Tbsp. coconut oil

1 cup cashews

1 cup pecans

½ cup nutritional yeast

½ tsp. sea salt

1) Heat the coconut oil in a large skillet. Add the cashews and pecans. Cook until golden brown, mixing often, for about 5 minutes.

2) Combine all of the ingredients in a food processor. Pulse until fine crumbles form. Enjoy!

DAIRY-FREE CHEESE SPREAD

This recipe was born out of my raw vegan days, when I discovered the creamy versatility of cashews. And thank goodness! It's wonderful to have a dairy- and soy-free alternative to cheese to use in baking, cooking, and snacking. I am hooked on this creamy, cheesy spread.

Quick Tip: A quick, savory snack that I often make with this Dairy-Free Cheese Spread is Zucchini Pizza Boats. Slice zucchinis in half, lengthwise, and scoop out some of the flesh. Fill with cheese spread and top with sliced olives, fresh basil, chopped pepperoni, and a drizzle of marinara sauce. Bake at 400°F for 20 minutes. Yum!

Prep: 15 minutes ❂ *Makes:* 16 servings

---

1 cup raw cashews

1 Tbsp. lemon juice

1 Tbsp. water

1 tsp. minced garlic

¼ cup olive oil

½ tsp. sea salt

¼ tsp. onion powder

¼ tsp. sweet paprika

dash of black pepper

---

1) Place the cashews in hot water. Soak for 10 minutes. Discard the water.

2) Combine all of the ingredients in a food processor. Pulse until smooth and creamy. Stop the blade and scrape the sides down every 30 seconds or so. This can take a while—be patient! If there are little pieces of cashew still visible, keep on blending. When it becomes wonderfully creamy, it's ready. Enjoy!

BBQ SAUCE

Here's the homemade BBQ sauce that I like to whip up. Since most store-bought BBQ sauces contain refined sugar and high fructose corn syrup, it's nice to have this quick and wholesome option.

Quick Tip: Making homemade ketchup is also quite easy. Here's how: Rub 5 large tomatoes and 1 large, peeled red onion with olive oil. Grill until charred—I use a grill pan over medium-high heat. Combine the charred tomatoes and onion in a food processor with 2 tablespoons tomato paste, 2 tablespoons apple cider vinegar, 1 packet stevia (or 3 tablespoons coconut palm sugar), 1 tablespoon Dijon mustard and 1 tablespoon lemon juice. Optionally, add a seeded, grilled jalapeño and a handful of fresh cilantro. Bend until smooth.

Prep: 5 minutes ❂ *Cook:* 8 minutes ❂ *Makes:* 1 cup

⅓ cup coconut palm sugar
⅔ cup organic, no-sugar-added ketchup
3 Tbsp. apple cider vinegar
2 tsp. Dijon mustard

1) Combine all of the ingredients in a small saucepan. Bring to a simmer over low heat, mixing often. Cook for 3 minutes and remove from heat. Enjoy!

DESSERTS

. . . the best for last

BIRTHDAY CAKE

Pull out your candles, party hat, and fun birthday napkins for this delicious slice of heaven! Birthdays and special occasions require a masterfully created cake to properly celebrate. That's my mantra, anyway. I took on the challenge to re-create our favorite birthday cake, using only wholesome, real food ingredients. The end result was a rich, moist cake filled with delicate sweet flavor and indulgent, dark chocolate frosting. It feels great to have a new, wholesome birthday cake tradition.

Don't get me wrong, this cake is an indulgence . . . big time. Yes, all the ingredients are wholesome, but it's still a very decadent, calorie-filled dessert, so watch portion size and limit this one for extra special occasions . . . like your next big birthday celebration!

Quick Tip: This recipe calls for turmeric, which may seem a bit strange. There's a good reason for it, don't worry! The turmeric gives the cake a vibrant yellow hue, without adding any detectable flavor. This is a little trick that I often use when I want to add yellow color to food without using artificial coloring. If you don't have turmeric, or don't care how yellow your cake turns out, feel free to leave the turmeric out. I promise it won't hurt my feelings. Much.

Prep: 20 minutes ❂ *Bake:* 25–30 minutes ❂ *Oven:* 350°F ❂ *Makes:* 1 cake

---

10 eggs, separated and divided

2 cups blanched almond flour

¼ cup coconut flour

½ tsp. baking soda

¼ tsp. turmeric

1 cup + 1 Tbsp. raw honey

1 Tbsp. vanilla extract

½ tsp. sea salt

1 batch Fluffy Chocolate Frosting (page 222)

1 batch Whipped Coconut Cream (page 218)

---

1) Preheat the oven to 350°F. Line an 8 × 2 round cake pan with parchment paper. Lightly brush with coconut oil.

2) In a medium bowl, combine the almond flour, coconut flour, baking soda, and turmeric.

3) Separate out 6 egg whites, and place the remaining yolks and eggs in a large mixing bowl. Add 1 cup of the honey and the vanilla extract to the egg yolk mixture. Mix well. Add the dry ingredients to the egg yolk mixture. Mix until creamy.

4) Whip the egg whites until soft peaks form. Add the remaining 1 tablespoon honey and ½ teaspoon salt to the whipped egg whites. Beat for 30 seconds. Carefully fold the egg whites into the batter with a large spoon. Batter should be fluffy.

5) Smooth the batter into the prepared pan. Bake for 25–30 minutes, until golden and baked through.

6) Once the cake has cooled, loosen the sides with a knife. Cover with a cake plate and flip the pan over. Carefully remove the pan and peel off the parchment paper. Use a serrated knife to slice the cake into two layers. Top the bottom cake layer with the Whipped Coconut Cream. Place the second cake layer on top of the Whipped Coconut Cream layer. Frost the entire cake with Fluffy Chocolate Frosting. Sneak a few licks . . . Once the frosting is smooth, place in the fridge to chill for at least 20 minutes, and preferably overnight. Slice and enjoy!

CHOCOLATE FUDGE CAKE

Do you love chocolate? Like really, really love chocolate? You're nodding your head yes, right? Okay, good, then we can be friends. If not, please check your pulse. This recipe is only for true chocolate lovers. And true friends.

Quick Tip: If this is just too much chocolate for you—chocolate overload—then another option is to frost this cake with Whipped Coconut Cream (page 218).

Prep: 20 minutes ❂ *Bake:* 25 minutes ❂ *Oven:* 350°F ❂ *Makes:* 2 cake rounds

---

1 cup dark chocolate

1 cup coconut oil

¾ cup raw honey

1½ cups blanched almond flour

1 tsp. sea salt

4 eggs

2 Tbsp. vanilla extract

½ tsp. almond extract

1 batch Fluffy Chocolate Frosting (page 222)

---

1) Preheat the oven to 350°F. Line two round 8-inch cake pans with parchment paper and grease the sides with coconut oil.

2) Combine the chocolate, coconut oil, and honey in a small saucepan. Place the saucepan in a skillet with an inch of water. Heat over medium. Mix constantly until smooth. Remove from heat and cool.

3) Combine the eggs and vanilla and almond extracts in a medium bowl. Add the cooled chocolate mixture.

4) Combine the almond flour and sea salt in another bowl. Add to the chocolate mixture. Mix well.

5) Fill the prepared pans with cake batter. Bake for 20 minutes, or until golden and cooked all the way through. Once the cake has cooled, chill for 15 minutes before frosting with Fluffy Chocolate Frosting. Enjoy that chocolate coma!

ANGEL FOOD CAKE

I grew up eating angel food cake all summer long. We would top it with sliced, locally grown strawberries and a dollop of whipped cream. This grain- and refined sugar-free version reminds me of those carefree summer days in the most delicious way.

Quick Tip: Angel food cakes are inverted after baking to prevent the cake from collapsing. This technique is necessary for all "foam cakes" that consist mainly of beaten egg whites and are void of fat or oil.

Prep: 20 minutes ❁ *Bake:* 35 minutes ❁ *Oven:* 325°F ❁ *Makes:* 1 cake

---

½ cup arrowroot starch

½ cup coconut flour

12 egg whites

1½ tsp. cream of tartar

1 tsp baking soda

¼ tsp sea salt

1 tsp vanilla extract

1 tsp almond extract

½ cup raw honey, melted

---

1) Preheat the oven to 325°F. Line the bottom of a tube pan with parchment paper. Lightly grease the sides with coconut oil.

2) Combine the arrowroot starch and coconut flour in a bowl. Mix with a whisk.

3) Gather 12 eggs. Separate the yolks from the whites. Use all those yolks to make something yummy like the Custard on page 216. Whip the egg whites with an electric whisk. Add the cream of tartar, baking soda, sea salt, and vanilla and almond extracts. Beat until stiff peaks form. Drizzle the honey in slowly.

4) Gently add the dry ingredients to the whipped egg mixture with a spatula.

5) Smooth the batter into the prepared tube pan. Bake for 35 minutes or until golden. Invert the pan and cool for 20 minutes. Time to enjoy some delicious angel food cake! Serve with Whipped Coconut Cream (page 218) and sliced strawberries.

FROSTED WATERMELON CAKE

Welcome to a whole new concept of cake! This Frosted Watermelon cake is made with sweet and refreshing watermelon, is frosted with coconut cream, and is decorated with melons, berries, and kiwis. It makes a stunning dessert that everyone will love to talk about. It's beautiful, sweet, and guilt free. Yes please—sign me up! I'll take two.

Quick Tip: Getting the coconut cream frosting to stick to the cake can be tricky . . . if you haven't properly chilled everything first. For best results, chill the shaped watermelon as well as the coconut cream frosting for at least 60 minutes before frosting. Smooth the frosting over the watermelon and then press sliced almonds all over the sides and decorate with blueberries and kiwis.

Prep: 30 minutes ✿ *Chill:* Overnight ✿ *Makes:* 12 servings

3 young coconuts

2 Tbsp. raw honey

1 tsp. vanilla extract

2 Tbsp. lemon juice

2 Tbsp. coconut oil

¼ tsp. sea salt

2 large, seedless watermelons

½ cup sliced almonds (or use shredded coconut)

2 kiwis, sliced

½ cup blueberries

1) Cut the tops off the young coconuts. Drain out the water but don't discard—drink it instead! Fresh coconut water is one of the tastiest drinks in the world. Scrape out the coconut meat and place it in a food processor. Add the honey, vanilla extract, lemon juice, coconut oil, and sea salt. Blend until the mixture becomes smooth. Place in the fridge to chill for 60 minutes.

2) Slice off the watermelon ends to create a flat base and top. Slice off all the green skin from the watermelon sides. Use the knife to smooth out the sides of your 'cake' to be as symmetrical as possible.

3) Stack the 2 watermelon cakes. Use the chilled frosting to carefully frost the entire cake. Lightly press the sliced almonds over the entire frosted cake. The almonds help to cover up any stubborn areas were the red watermelon shows through.

4) Decorate with the sliced almonds, blueberries, and kiwi slices. Chill to firm the frosting. Slice and enjoy!

CARAMEL APPLE PIE

Why make apple pie when you could make *caramel* apple pie? It just makes sense. Growing up in the great state of Washington, I have eaten and picked my fair share of apples. Or probably more than my fair share. As they say, an apple a day keeps the doctor away!

Quick Tip: So what do you do when you are seriously craving apple pie, but you need it to be ready in 10 minutes flat? You make skillet apple pie, of course. Here's how: Melt 1 tablespoon coconut oil in a skillet. Add 3 chopped apples. Cook for 5 minutes, stirring often until soft. Add 2 teaspoons ground cinnamon, a pinch of nutmeg, a pinch of sea salt, 2 tablespoons raisins, and ¼ ground walnuts. Cook for another 3 minutes and serve hot.

Prep: 45 minutes ❂ *Bake:* 45 minutes ❂ *Oven:* 375°F ❂ *Makes:* 8 servings

6 green apples

½ + ½ cup coconut palm sugar

¼ cup + ½ cup blanched almond flour

¼ + ¼ tsp. sea salt

1 lemon

1 Pie Crust (page 188)

½ cup palm shortening

½ cup sliced almonds

½ cup Caramel Sauce (page 220)

Vanilla Ice Cream (page 210)

1) Preheat the oven to 375°F.

2) Peel, core, and slice the apples. Juice the lemon and toss with the apple slices.

3) Combine ½ cup coconut palm sugar, ½ cup blanched almond flour, ¼ teaspoon sea salt, and lemon in a large bowl. Add the sliced apples and mix well. Fill your pre-baked pie crust with the coated apple slices.

4) Combine the palm shortening, sliced almonds, ½ cup coconut palm sugar, ½ cup blanched almond flour, and ¼ teaspoon sea salt in a large bowl. Mix well. Sprinkle the almond mixture over the pie.

5) Cover the pie tightly with foil. Bake for 25 minutes. Remove the foil, bake for another 20 minutes. Remove the pie from the oven and drizzle with the caramel sauce. Serve with large scoops of Vanilla Ice Cream (page 210). Enjoy!

KEY LIME PIE

This Key Lime Pie is light, tangy, and refreshing. Serve it up chilled with a dollop of Whipped Coconut Cream. Yes, please!

Quick Tip: Emotional eating temporarily relieves distress . . . and then makes it impossible to achieve what you really want. Part of your real food journey is learning how to have a healthy relationship with food by not using food as a solution to emotional pain. It's easier said than done, my friend, but it is possible. Having a slice of Key Lime Pie with our friends and family as we celebrate life is a whole different animal than eating an entire pie alone because our heart hurts. Eat to celebrate life, not to escape it.

Prep: 15 minutes ❁ *Bake:* 15 minutes ❁ *Oven:* 350°F ❁ *Makes:* 12 servings

---

6 limes
2 egg yolks
1 cup Sweetened Condensed Coconut Milk (page 224)
1 Graham Crust (page 186)
Whipped Coconut Cream (page 218)

---

1) Combine 1 tablespoon lime zest, ½ cup lime juice, the egg yolks, and the Sweetened Condensed Coconut Milk in a food processor. Blend until smooth.

2) Pour the mixture into a Graham Crust. Bake for 15 minutes. Cool and chill for 60 minutes. Serve with Whipped Coconut Cream. Enjoy!

GRAHAM CRUST

Okay, this crust doesn't contain any graham crackers whatsoever. So why did I name it Graham Crust? Well, this crust is as close to a graham cracker crust as I've been able to make using wholesome, grain-free ingredients. Use it in exchange for a traditional graham cracker crust in your favorite desserts.

Quick Tip: If you don't eat right, neither will your children. This is my big reason why I cook healthy food. I do it so that my children will learn healthy eating habits. I do it so that their bodies will be healthy and free of weight-related ailments and disease. Why do you cook healthy foods? What's your big reason why?

Prep: 10 minutes ❀ *Bake:* 12 minutes ❀ *Oven:* 400°F ❀ *Makes:* 1 crust

---

1½ cups raw pecans
¼ tsp. sea salt
¾ cup dates, pitted
3 Tbsp. coconut oil

---

1) Preheat the oven to 400°F. Lightly grease a pie dish with coconut oil.

2) Combine all of the ingredients in a food processor. Pulse until the pecans and dates are fully incorporated into the dough. Transfer the dough into the pie pan. Use your fingers to press the dough evenly over the dish.

3) Bake for 12 minutes, until golden. Fill with your favorite pie filling—Key Lime Pie (page 184) or Custard (page 216). Chill for 30 minutes. Enjoy!

PIE CRUST

Here's a pie crust that's a grain- and dairy-free alternative to traditional pie crusts. Sure, it takes more effort than simply purchasing a frozen pie crust from the store, but this one is better for you. Fill it with your favorite seasonal fruit!

Quick Tip: Changing your diet is much more possible than you may believe. It IS possible to eat healthy food without feeling deprived, while feeling well nourished and satisfied.

But first it requires a commitment on your part. Give up the junk. Decide here and now that you are DONE with it. It may taste good while you are eating it, but it's hurting you, so stop. Open yourself up to the possibility that you ARE capable of eating healthy as a way of life.

I know you can do this, because I've been where you are and I've done it myself. How exciting to know that a whole new healthy life awaits you!

You'll love how the new you feels. (And I'll be super proud of you too!)

Prep: 20 minutes ❁ *Bake:* 12 minutes ❁ *Oven:* 400°F ❁ *Makes:* 1 crust

---

½ cup blanched almond flour

½ cup coconut flour

¼ cup arrowroot starch

¼ tsp. sea salt

½ cup coconut oil, frozen and grated

2 Tbsp. cold water

1 egg

½ tsp. apple cider vinegar

---

1) Preheat the oven to 400°F. Lightly grease a pie dish with coconut oil.

2) Combine the almond flour, coconut flour, arrowroot starch and sea salt in a bowl. Mix well.

3) Use a cheese grater to grate the frozen coconut oil into little pieces over the dough. Mix with your fingers until dough forms.

4) Combine the water, egg, and vinegar in a small bowl. Add to the dough. Mix in with your fingers. Form the dough into a ball. Cover with plastic wrap and chill for at least 30 minutes, and for up to 3 days. Remove from the fridge and let sit for 20 minutes before using.

5) Place the dough ball on a piece of parchment paper and cover with another piece of parchment paper. Use a rolling pin to flatten the dough. Shape the dough into a flat circle the size of your pie dish. Pick the parchment paper up and invert the dough into the pie dish. Press the dough into the dish. Fix any broken pieces and cracks by pressing the dough back together with your fingers. Pinch the edges to form a pretty crust.

6) Bake for 8–12 minutes, until golden. Fill with your favorite filling and return to the oven for another 10 minutes, or until bubbly. Enjoy!

CARAMEL-FROSTED COOKIES

With my *very* helpful six year old, Chloe, underfoot in my kitchen these days, I'm always coming up with recipes that she can assist with. Cookies are her favorite—she is a cookie-shaping champion. This recipe is extra fun because there is frosting to spread and nuts to sprinkle!

Quick Tip: Dates are a nutritious sweetener and a wonderful substitute for refined sugar. This caramel frosting is sweetened solely with dates. Try it and see how awesomely sweet it tastes. Many recipes can be modified to use ground dates to replace the added sweetener. I like to say that dates are nature's candy!

Prep: 20 minutes ✿ *Bake:* 8 minutes ✿ *Oven:* 350°F ✿ *Makes:* 12 cookies

2 cups blanched almond flour

¼ tsp. + 1 pinch sea salt

¼ tsp. baking soda

1 tsp. ground cinnamon

¼ cup palm shortening

2 Tbsp. raw honey

1 Tbsp. + 1 tsp. vanilla extract

20 dates, pitted

3 Tbsp. water

5 Tbsp. canned coconut milk, full fat

¼ cup pecans, chopped

1) Preheat the oven to 350°F. Line a baking sheet with parchment paper.

2) Combine the almond flour, ¼ teaspoon sea salt, baking soda, and cinnamon in a food processor. Pulse to combine. Add the palm shortening, honey, and 1 tablespoon vanilla extract. Pulse to form sticky dough.

3) Shape the dough into 12 cookies. Place on the prepared baking sheet. Bake for 8 minutes, until golden.

4) Soak the dates in hot water for 15 minutes. Drain.

5) Combine the dates, remaining teaspoon vanilla, the water, coconut milk, and a pinch of salt in a food processor. Blend into a smooth frosting. This takes a while! If you can see pieces of date, then it's not ready, so keep on blending.

6) Once the cookies have cooled, frost and sprinkle with chopped pecans. Enjoy!

CHOCOLATE CHIP BRAZIL NUT COOKIES

Here is a brand-new version of my popular Caveman Cookies recipe . . . and I have to say, it's pretty awesome. It sure was hard not to share this recipe with you online months ago, but somehow I managed. Now that the wait is over, don't waste another minute—go make these cookies immediately!

Quick Tip: Did you know that Brazil nuts are actually seeds? Or at least, that's what Google says. I find that the addition of ground Brazil nuts (seeds?) in these cookies gives it a delicate, smooth texture. That being said, you can really use whatever nuts you like. Feel free to substitute with almond, walnut, pecan, or sunflower seeds.

Prep: 20 minutes ✸ *Bake:* 12 minutes ✸ *Oven:* 350°F ✸ *Makes:* 12 cookies

---

1½ cups raw Brazil nuts

3 Tbsp. coconut flour

½ cup blanched almond flour

2 Tbsp. arrowroot starch

1 tsp. baking soda

¼ tsp. sea salt

1 egg

¼ cup raw honey (add another 2 Tbsp. for sweeter cookies)

3 Tbsp. coconut oil

½ cup mini chocolate chips or chopped dark chocolate

---

1) Preheat the oven to 350°F. Line a baking sheet with parchment paper.

2) Pulse the Brazil nuts in a food processor until a fine powder forms. Add the coconut flour, almond flour, arrowroot starch, baking soda, and sea salt. Pulse to combine. Add the egg, honey, and coconut oil. Pulse to form sticky dough. Mix the chocolate chips in with a spoon.

3) Shape into 12 large cookies, or 20 small cookies. Place the cookies on the prepared baking sheet. Bake for 12 minutes, or until evenly brown. Serve with chilled coconut milk. Enjoy!

CHOCOLATE COCONUT COOKIES

These are arguably the best cookies that I've ever made. With simple, wholesome ingredients, and the classic chocolate and coconut flavor combination, I've yet to meet someone who didn't love these. So consider yourself warned. Make extras. Lots of extras.

Quick Tip: I like to store these cookies in the freezer. Take them out about 10 minutes before serving.

Prep: 15 minutes ✿ *Bake:* 30 minutes ✿ *Oven:* 300°F ✿ *Makes:* 15 cookies

---

2 cups unsweetened, shredded coconut

1 cup blanched almond flour

¼ tsp. sea salt

½ cup + 2 Tbsp. coconut oil

½ cup coconut palm sugar

1 tsp. vanilla extract

¼ tsp. almond extract

2 eggs, beaten

¾ cup dark chocolate pieces

---

1) Preheat the oven to 300°F. Line a baking sheet with parchment paper.

2) Combine the shredded coconut, almond flour, and sea salt in a bowl. Mix well.

3) In another bowl, beat the eggs. Add the ½ cup coconut oil, coconut palm sugar, vanilla extract, and almond extract. Mix well. Add the dry ingredients to the wet ones. Mix until fully incorporated.

4) Shape the dough into 15 cookies. Place on the prepared baking sheet. Bake for 30 minutes, until golden. Chill the cookies for 20 minutes.

5) Place the chocolate and remaining 2 tablespoons coconut oil in a small saucepan. Place the saucepan in a medium skillet filled with an inch of water. Turn the heat on medium-low and stir often while the mixture becomes smooth.

6) Cover a large plate with parchment paper. Dip the cookies in the melted chocolate and place on the prepared plate. Drizzle chocolate over the top. Place back in the fridge for 15 minutes, until the chocolate hardens. Enjoy!

ZUCCHINI BROWNIES

Hmmmmm, what to do with all the zucchini from the garden?

Make brownies?!? Yes! This recipe is so much fun. Zucchini adds moisture and is virtually undetectable.

Quick Tip: Don't give up. Hang in there. Make healthy choices one day at a time. You'll achieve your goal if you simply never stop striving toward it.

Prep: 25 minutes ✿ *Bake:* 25 minutes ✿ *Oven:* 350°F ✿ *Makes:* 16 brownies

---

½ cup dark chocolate, chopped

¼ cup coconut oil

¼ cup raw honey

2 eggs

2 tsp. vanilla extract

¼ tsp. almond extract

1 cup blanched almond flour

¼ cup unsweetened cocoa powder

1½ tsp. baking soda

¼ tsp. sea salt

2 zucchini

---

1) Preheat the oven to 350°F. Line an 8 × 8 baking pan with parchment paper and grease the sides with coconut oil.

2) Combine dark chocolate, coconut oil, and honey in a small saucepan. Place the saucepan in a medium skillet filled with an inch of water. Turn the heat on medium-low and stir often as the mixture becomes smooth.

3) Combine the eggs and extracts in a small bowl. Combine the flour, cocoa powder, baking soda, and salt in a medium bowl. Mix well. Add the dry ingredients to the wet ones. Mix until fully incorporated.

4) Shred the zucchini in a food processor using a grating attachment. Place the shredded zucchini in the center of a clean dish towel. Twist the towel and squeeze. Yep, zucchini juice is green. Return the shredded zucchini to a cutting board. Mince very finely. You want these zucchini pieces to be really tiny—this makes it impossible to detect that the finished brownies contain zucchini. Sneaky, sneaky mom. Mix the minced zucchini to the brownie batter.

5) Spread the batter into your prepared baking pan. Bake for 25 minutes, or until fully set and cooked all the way through. Now have fun serving these delicious zucchini brownies to unsuspecting recipients. Enjoy!

MINI BROWNIES

The happiest moments in my adolescent years were making boxed brownies with my bestie, Alison. We had a standing sleepover and brownie making session every Friday night. Oh, the good ole days. While my love for brownies is still going strong, I no longer can tolerate the sickly sweetness of packaged brownies.

So here's the perfect brownie alternative to boxed brownie mixes. Everyone who has tried these has loved them . . . these brownies are that good. I love the idea of making brownies in a mini muffin tin because it forces portion control. One little morsel is really all you need to satisfy your sweet tooth. When I have a pan of brownies in front of me it's hard to just cut a little square and be done with it . . . the squares keep getting bigger and bigger.

Quick Tip: This recipe does call for ¾ cup of raw honey, in order to make it taste nearly as sweet as traditional brownies. Feel free to reduce the amount of honey, but if you're baking these to share, I'd keep it pretty close to that amount.

Prep: 20 minutes ✿ *Bake:* 25 minutes ✿ *Oven:* 350°F ✿ *Makes:* 48 mini brownies

---

1 cup dark chocolate

1 cup coconut oil

¾ cup raw honey

1½ cups blanched almond flour

1 tsp. sea salt

4 eggs

2 Tbsp. vanilla extract

½ tsp. almond extract

1 cup mini chocolate chips **For Double Chocolate Brownies

1 cup unsweetened, shredded coconut **For Coconut Brownies

1 cup Fluffy Chocolate Frosting (page 222)

---

1) Preheat the oven to 350°F. Lightly grease a mini muffin pan with coconut oil, or line with paper liners.

2) Combine the chocolate, coconut oil, and raw honey in a small saucepan. Place the saucepan in a skillet with an inch of water. Heat over medium. Mix constantly until smooth.

3) In a medium bowl, combine the almond flour and sea salt. In a large bowl, combine the eggs and vanilla and almond extracts. Add the dry ingredients to the wet ingredients and mix well.

4) For Double Chocolate Brownies: add a cup of mini chocolate chips.

5) For Coconut Brownies: add a cup of unsweetened shredded coconut. I find it fun to separate the batter in half and to mix chocolate into half and coconut into the other half. Or mix the chocolate and the coconut into all the batter.

6) Fill each mini muffin tin with brownie batter. Bake for 20–25 minutes, until set and cooked through. If you are feeling really chocolatey, frost with Fluffy Chocolate Frosting. Enjoy!

CHEESECAKE BITES

It may sound strange to have a cheesecake bar that's dairy free, but you've gotta trust me on this one. Soaked cashews combined in the food processor with coconut oil, raw honey, vanilla, and lemon juice make a creamy, delicious cheesecake bar. Throw in a crust made with almond flour and dates, then top it with fresh strawberries, and you've got one seriously nutritious, amazing-tasting dessert.

Quick Tip: A fun variation on this recipe is to top the bites with date-sweetened caramel frosting, rather than fruit. In a food processor, blend 20 dates (soaked for an hour in hot water, and then drained), 3 tablespoons water, 5 tablespoons full-fat coconut milk, 1 teaspoon vanilla, and a pinch of sea salt. Blend on high until creamy—have patience, this takes awhile.

Prep: 40 minutes ✹ *Soak:* 2 hours ✹ *Makes:* 24 mini bites

---

2 cups raw cashews

½ cup raw honey

2 Tbsp. + ½ cup coconut oil

1 tsp. vanilla extract

1 tsp. lemon juice

1 cup blanched almond flour

¼ tsp. sea salt

½ cup dates, pitted

24 raspberries

24 mint leaves

---

1) Cover the cashews with filtered water and soak for 2 hours. Drain and rinse.

2) Combine the almond flour, sea salt, and dates in a food processor. Pulse until an even powder forms. Add the coconut oil. Pulse to create a sticky dough.

3) Line a 24 mini muffin pan with paper liners. Drop 1 tablespoon of dough into each liner. Firmly press the dough down.

4) Combine the cashews, honey, ½ cup coconut oil, vanilla extract, and lemon juice in a food processor. Blend until creamy and smooth. This can take a while, so be patient! Go take a bath, read a book, run a marathon . . .

5) Fill a piping bag with the cashew mixture. Top each crust with a generous serving of the cashew cream. Decorate with fresh raspberries and mint leaves. Chill for 20 minutes before serving. Enjoy!

CHOCOLATE COCONUT CASHEWS

It was a sparkling blue day in Maui, and we had spent an hour hiking down to the Nakalele blowhole. The kids ran ahead, hopping from rock to rock like nimble mountain goats. The sun was on our backs, sweat turning our tank tops a darker shade . . . we were all hungry. At the highway a jovial local couple greeted us from under the shade of their roadside stand. Would we like cold water and to sample their chocolate cashews? But of course. One taste of the chocolate-covered cashew and coconut mixture, and we were hooked. This recipe is my rendition of the sweet and salty Maui treat.

Quick Tip: When selecting dark chocolate, always choose one that is 73 percent cocoa content or higher. The higher the cocoa content, the lower the sugar content. If you're new to dark chocolate, it may take a little while to modify your palate from uber sweet milk chocolate, but soon anything lower than 73 percent cocoa will taste sickly sweet.

Prep: 20 minutes ❁ *Cook:* 12 minutes ❁ *Makes:* 4 servings

1 cup raw, unsalted cashews

¼ cup coconut oil, divided

1 cup unsweetened coconut flakes

¼ tsp. sea salt

1 cup dark chocolate

¼ tsp. almond extract

1) Place a large skillet over medium heat. Add 2 tablespoons coconut oil. Add the cashews to the skillet. Cook, mixing often, for 5 minutes. Add the coconut flakes and salt to the skillet. When the cashews and coconut flakes are toasted, remove from heat.

2) Place the chocolate, coconut oil and almond extract in a small pot and place that pot in a medium skillet with an inch of water. Place over medium-low heat, stirring often until the chocolate mixture is smooth. In a large bowl, combine the toasted cashews, coconut flakes, and melted chocolate.

3) Line a rimmed baking sheet with parchment paper. Spread the chocolate mixture over the rimmed baking sheet. Place the baking sheet in the fridge for 30 minutes. Take a big spoon and break up the mixture every 10 minutes to prevent large pieces from sticking together. Enjoy!

COCONUT CANDY

My grandma, Mary Ella Tway Dorman Pinto, in addition to having the longest, coolest name I've ever heard, shared my love for sweets. She kept boxes of assorted See's candy truffles in her freezer and would pull them out for an after dinner treat. She would turn the candy over and poke the bottom to get a glimpse of the filling, then would put half of them back in the box! Oh, the things adorable little ladies over eighty can get away with . . . I now keep a container of these coconut candies in my freezer, a habit that Mary Ella Tway Dorman Pinto is surely smiling down on me for.

Quick Tip: The freezer is important in getting these candies to stick together. It's all held together by chilled coconut oil, which becomes solid when cold. That's why it's a good idea to keep these sweet morsels in the freezer. Also, these are easy to hide in the freezer, so you won't have to share as many!

Prep: 20 minutes ❀ *Makes:* 16 candies

---

2 cups unsweetened shredded coconut

¼ cup raw honey

1 Tbsp. coconut flour

¼ cup blanched almond flour

¼ cup, plus 1 Tbsp. coconut oil, divided

¼ tsp. sea salt

16 raw almonds

½ cup dark chocolate

---

1) Combine the shredded coconut, honey, coconut flour, almond flour, ¼ cup coconut oil, and sea salt in a bowl. Mix well. Place in the freezer for 5 minutes.

2) Line an 8 × 8 pan with parchment paper. Press the coconut mixture into the prepared pan. Place the pan in the freezer for 5 minutes.

4) Place 1 tablespoon coconut oil and ½ cup dark chocolate in a small pot. Place the pot in a medium skillet over medium heat. Mix until smooth.

 5) Place the almonds in even rows over the coconut mixture. Pour a spoonful of melted chocolate over each almond. Place the pan in the freezer for 5 minutes. Cut the candy into 4 pieces. Use the edges of the parchment paper to pull the pieces out of the pan and onto a cutting board. Cut each piece into 4, so you end up with 16 pieces. Store in the freezer. Enjoy!

ICE CREAM SANDWICH

This is, hands down, our favorite summertime snack. I love the idea of calling frozen bananas ice cream. When you really compare the consistency and sweetness of frozen banana to actual ice cream, it's not that far off. So in this awesomely simple recipe, I took half of a banana, filled it with an almond butter mixture, and covered it in dark chocolate. It's simple, quick, easy, and downright delicious.

The kids loved the novelty of eating this treat on a stick, and I loved the convenience of keeping a bunch in the freezer and simply grabbing a couple and giving them to the kids with the instructions of "Go eat these outside!"

Quick Tip: One of my favorite healthy eating quotes to share on Facebook is, "If your food can go bad, then it's good for you. If your food can't go bad, then it's bad for you." The concept is simple and profound. Of course someone then inevitably chimes in, "Except for honey!" Yes, smarty pants, except for honey.

Prep: 15 minutes ❀ *Freeze:* 40 minutes ❀ *Makes:* 8 servings

⅔ cup almond butter

1 tsp. vanilla extract

¼ tsp. almond extract

½ tsp. ground cinnamon

⅔ cup dark chocolate

2 Tbsp. coconut oil

4 bananas

8 wooden sticks

1) Combine the almond butter, vanilla extract, almond extract, and ground cinnamon in a bowl. Mix well.

2) Place the chocolate and coconut oil in a small saucepan. Place the saucepan in a skillet with 1 inch of water over medium heat. Stir often as the chocolate melts and becomes smooth. Remove from heat. Cool slightly.

3) Peel the bananas. Cut in half lengthwise and crosswise. Rub the almond mixture on the cut side of each banana. Sandwich the halves together on top of a wooden stick. Place the banana sandwiches on a freezer safe tray lined with parchment paper. Freeze for 30 minutes.

4) Dip each frozen sandwich in the melted chocolate. Place back on the parchment paper and freeze for 10 additional minutes, until the chocolate is firm. Enjoy!

PASSION FRUIT SORBET

My in-laws, Joe and Suzy, have the greenest thumbs of anyone I know. Their cozy backyard, in Anaheim, California, produces every kind of fruit and vegetable that you could imagine. There are cucumbers, tomatoes, peppers, raspberries, strawberries, figs, lemons, oranges, persimmons, grapefruit, avocados, grapes, and guavas. Most recently they have taken to growing passion fruit.

Passion fruit, also known as purple granadilla, grows on vines with the oval, purple fruit hanging by the dozens under large green leaves. The small, but flavorful, fruit is a nutritional powerhouse containing vitamin C, pro-vitamin A, beta carotene, fiber, iron, and potassium. But, more important for this recipe, the fruit pulp has this refreshing, sweet-tangy flavor that's perfect for a cool treat.

Quick Tip: You'll notice that this sorbet is fruit only. Zero sweeteners. Rather than use any sweetener, I decided to make this sorbet a 50–50 split between tangy passion fruit and sweet ripe mango. The result is refreshingly sweet. Whenever you can in your cooking, reduce the amount of added sweeteners. I'm always surprised at how much better naturally sweetened desserts taste compared to refined sugar-loaded desserts.

Prep: 15 minutes ✿ *Freeze:* 2 hours ✿ *Makes:* 6 servings

½ cup passion fruit pulp (from 6–8 passion fruits)

1 cup mango, diced

1 cup mango-orange juice (fruit only)

2 egg whites

---

1) Slice open the passion fruit and scoop out the pulp. Peel, seed, and dice the mango.

2) In a freezer-safe bowl, combine the passion fruit pulp, diced mango, and juice. At this point you have the option to blend the mixture for a smoother sorbet, or leave it with fruit chunks. I like the chunks. Put the fruit mixture in the freezer for an hour.

3) Whip the egg whites until stiff peaks form. Fold the egg white mixture into the fruit mixture. Freeze for another hour.

4) Mix again and freeze for additional 10 minute increments if needed. Enjoy!

VANILLA ICE CREAM

Here's a very quick and easy recipe for Vanilla Ice Cream that's dairy- and refined sugar-free. My kids love to eat this ice cream topped with fresh, sliced fruit.

Quick Tip: Did you slip up on your diet yesterday? Eat something you know you shouldn't have, or eaten more than you should have? Shake it off. Today is a brand-new day and a clean slate. 1. Drink more water. 2. Eat more greens. 3. Say no to sugar. 4. Repeat.

Prep: 10 minutes ✿ *Freeze:* 15 minutes ✿ *Makes:* 4 servings

---

2 (13.66-oz.) cans coconut milk, full fat

2 frozen bananas

3 Tbsp. coconut palm sugar

1 Tbsp. vanilla extract

---

1) Chill the cans of coconut milk in the fridge overnight. Do NOT shake the cans up at all! Ever! Carefully turn the cans over and open from the bottom. Drain out the liquid and scoop the white cream into a blender. Discard the liquid.

2) Combine all of the ingredients in the blender. Blend until smooth.

3) Pour the vanilla mixture into an ice cream maker. Turn the ice cream maker on and run for about 15 minutes, until creamy. I've found that coconut milk based ice cream takes less time than dairy based ice cream to freeze— thanks to the way coconut hardens when cold. Enjoy!

MINT CHIP ICE CREAM

I absolutely love the taste of mint and chocolate! In my former life as a sugar addict, I would eat York Peppermint Patties like they were going out of style. This light and refreshing Mint Chip Ice Cream recipe is made with coconut milk, frozen bananas, and a touch of coconut palm sugar. It's pretty awesome.

Quick Tip: If you also love the taste of mint and chocolate, then here's a tasty way to liven up your next protein shake. In a blender, combine: 1 cup ice, ½ a frozen banana, 1 tablespoon dark chocolate—chopped, 1 cup water, 1 scoop high quality chocolate protein powder, and 2 drops peppermint extract.

Prep: 10 minutes ✺ *Freeze:* 15 minutes ✺ *Makes:* 4 servings

---

2 (13.66-oz.) cans coconut milk, full fat

2 frozen bananas

3 Tbsp. coconut palm sugar

1 Tbsp. vanilla extract

2 tsp. peppermint extract

⅓ cup mini chocolate chips

---

1) Chill the cans of coconut milk in the fridge overnight. Do NOT shake the cans up at all! Ever! Carefully turn the cans over and open from the bottom. Drain out the liquid and scoop the white cream into a blender. Discard the liquid.

2) Combine the bananas, coconut palm sugar, vanilla, and peppermint extracts in the blender. Blend until smooth.

3) Pour the ice cream mixture into an ice cream maker. Turn the ice cream maker on and run for about 15 minutes, until creamy. Add the mini chocolate chips just as it becomes creamy. Enjoy!

FROZEN HOT CHOCOLATE

I don't know about you, but I have a weakness for sweet, chilly, blended drinks—especially ones that involve chocolate and whipped cream. Yummmm. The problem with traditional frozen hot chocolate (and most sweet, blended drinks) is all that refined sugar and dairy. Think of them as sugar bombs. Sugar bombs that wreck havoc. You don't want any part of that. You do, however, deserve a wholesome, delightful glass of this dairy- and refined sugar-free frozen hot chocolate.

Quick Tip: Call me a lazy cook (or lazy chef . . . sounds cooler) but I just don't have the time for double boilers. I don't have time for *any* fancy schmancy equipment for that matter. The lazy chef's double boiler is to simply put some water in a skillet and then place a pot directly in the skillet. Voila. That was easy. And now our precious chocolate will not burn. Ah, life is good.

Prep: 10 minutes ✿ *Cook*: 10 minutes ✿ *Makes*: 6 servings

⅓ cup dark chocolate, 73% (or higher) cocoa content, chopped

2 tsp. unsweetened cocoa powder

1 Tbsp. raw honey

1½ cups canned coconut milk, full fat

3 cups ice

½ cup Whipped Coconut Cream (page 218)

---

1) Gather the dark chocolate, unsweetened cocoa powder, raw honey, and coconut milk.

2) Fill a medium skillet partially with water and place over medium-low heat. Place a small pot in the skillet and fill with the dark chocolate. Stir often until the chocolate melts.

3) Add the unsweetened cocoa powder and raw honey to the melted chocolate. Continue to stir often until the mixture becomes smooth.

4) Add ½ cup of the coconut milk to the melted chocolate mixture. Mix until smooth and then remove from heat. Allow the mixture to cool to room temperature.

5) Pour the chocolate mixture into a high-speed blender. Add the ice.

6) Blend on high until smooth and creamy. Pour into chilled glasses and top with a dollop of Whipped Coconut Cream and a fresh raspberry. Enjoy!

CUSTARD

Custard is love in food form. It's sweet, creamy, and gives you a hug from the inside. I came up with this recipe to use up leftover egg yolks from my Fluffy Egg White Biscuits recipe. It has since become one of our favorite summertime desserts, eaten chilled with fresh berries on top.

Quick Tip: It's important that your custard does not come to a boil in step 4 or it could curdle. Curdled custard is not cute. Not cute at all.

Prep: 10 minutes ❂ *Cook:* 15 minutes ❂ *Makes:* 8 servings

8 egg yolks

1 cup raw honey

1 Tbsp. coconut flour

3 (13.66-oz.) cans coconut milk, full fat

1 tsp. vanilla extract

1 lemon, zest

1) Separate the yolks from the whites. Use the whites for something awesome, like Fluffy Egg White Biscuits (page 154) or Angel Food Cake (page 178). Or make yourself a yummy egg white omelet with bacon. Mmmmmm, bacon.

2) Combine the egg yolks and honey in a saucepan. Whisk together until smooth. Mix in the coconut flour.

3) Combine the coconut milk, vanilla extract, and lemon zest in a medium saucepan. Place the milk mixture over medium heat. Bring to a boil and then remove from the heat.

4) Pour the hot milk mixture into the egg yolk mixture, stirring while you pour. Place the mixture on low heat, stirring constantly for 5 minutes. Don't boil; just simmer.

5) Remove from heat and cool for a few minutes. Continue to stir occasionally as it cools. Once cooled to room temperature, pour into individual custard cups. Chill in the fridge for 30 minutes or until serving. Garnish with fresh fruit and mint leaves. Enjoy!

Keuilian

WHIPPED COCONUT CREAM

There are so many things that simply require a white, whipped accompaniment. Waffles, frozen hot chocolate, angel food cake, strawberries, coconut ice cream sundaes . . . this list inadequate but I'm afraid we've run out of space. You get the idea. Giving up dairy and refined sugar doesn't mean we have given up the need for whipped cream. I scream. You scream. We all scream for whipped cream.

Quick Tip: The key to successfully making this *whipped* cream, and not *soggy* cream, is to properly drain the coconut milk. Here's how:

- Don't shake the can of coconut milk—this combines the liquid and cream that we are trying to separate.

- Chill the cans of coconut milk overnight.

- Carefully remove the cans from the fridge and turn upside down. Use a can opener to remove the bottom of the can.

- Pour out the liquid.

- Scoop out the white coconut cream that's left in the can.

Prep: 15 minutes ❁ *Chill:* overnight ❁ *Makes:* 4 servings

---

2 (13.66-oz.) cans coconut milk, full fat

¼ cup raw honey

1 Tbsp. vanilla extract

½ tsp. almond extract

1 Tbsp. coconut oil

pinch of sea salt

---

1) Chill the cans of coconut milk in the fridge overnight. Do NOT shake the cans up at all! Ever! Carefully turn the cans over and open from the bottom. Drain out the liquid and scoop the white cream into a bowl. Discard the liquid.

2) Combine all of the ingredients in a mixing bowl. Beat with an electric whisk. Whip until creamy. Keep chilled. Enjoy!

CARAMEL SAUCE

Most caramel apple recipes call for loads of refined sugar and corn syrup. That's not RHR approved, so after some trial and error, I came up with the perfect equation of coconut palm sugar to create that delicious caramel-y flavor.

Quick Tip: What to do with your caramel sauce?

> Make caramel apples.
>
> Drizzle over Caramel Apple Pie (page 182)
>
> Use as a dip for green apple slices.
>
> Drizzle over Vanilla Ice Cream (page 210).
>
> Put a little in your hair if you're having a bad day.

Prep: 5 minutes ❁ **Cook:** 20 minutes ❁ **Makes:** 1 cup

---

1 cup coconut palm sugar

¼ cup + 1 Tbsp. canned coconut milk, full fat

4 Tbsp. coconut oil

1 Tbsp. vanilla extract

pinch of sea salt

½ tsp. baking soda

---

1) Combine the coconut palm sugar, coconut milk, coconut oil, vanilla extract, and sea salt in a skillet. Mix well and place over medium high heat. Bring the mixture to a boil, reduce to low heat, and continue to cook, stirring often, for 5 minutes.

2) Temporarily remove the skillet from heat. Whisk in the baking soda. The caramel will turn a lighter color and will become creamy.

3) Return to low heat. Cook, mixing often, for 2 minutes. Allow to cool and thicken for 5 minutes before using. Store in the fridge. Enjoy!

FLUFFY CHOCOLATE FROSTING

You are what you eat. And I'm a big bowl of Fluffy Chocolate Frosting.

Quick Tip: Temperature plays an important role in making this frosting perfectly creamy and fluffy. As does the electric mixer. Once you've melted everything in step 2, the frosting goes into the freezer for 5 minutes. Then we beat the frosting (what did it ever do to us?) with an electric mixer. Next the frosting goes back into the freezer for another time out. Then back to the beating. You will know when the frosting has hit that creamy, fluffy turning point because it will turn a lighter shade of brown. And at that point you can stop beating it. Geesh.

Prep: 20 minutes ✺ *Makes:* 4 cups

2 cups dark chocolate
½ cup canned coconut milk, full fat
½ cup coconut oil
½ cup palm shortening
½ cup raw honey

1) In a double boiler (or a lazy chef's saucepan-skillet boiler!), Melt all of the ingredients together. Mix often until smooth. Remove from heat and place in the freezer for 5 minutes.

2) Beat the chocolate frosting with an electric mixer. Place back in the freezer for 5 minutes and beat again. Continue this process until the frosting thickens and becomes creamy. Enjoy!

SWEETENED CONDENSED COCONUT MILK

Here's a more wholesome alternative to traditional, store bought sweetened condensed milk. It's quite simple to make, just takes a little patience as you stir, stir, stir, stir.

Quick Tip: How should you use this Sweetened Condensed Coconut Milk? Hmmm, let me count the ways:

1. Make Key Lime Pie. Recipe on page 184.

2. Add a spoonful to your morning coffee.

3. Dip your Pretzel Bites in it. Recipe on page 70.

4. Spread some over a piece of Almond Bread. Recipe on page 142.

5. Put some in your hair . . . ? Maybe not.

Prep: 10 minutes ❂ *Cook:* 40 minutes ❂ *Makes:* 1 cup

2 (13.66-oz.) cans coconut milk, full fat
⅓ cup raw honey

1) Chill the cans of coconut milk in the fridge overnight. Do NOT shake the cans up at all! Ever! Carefully turn the cans over and open from the bottom. Drain out the liquid and scoop the white cream into a bowl. Discard the liquid.

2) Combine the coconut cream and honey in a skillet. Place over low heat. Cook and stir as the cream and honey melt.

3) Use a whisk to gently stir. Cook for about 40 minutes, stirring often. The mixture will reduce by half to become thick. Store in an airtight container in the fridge and use in a tasty dessert. Enjoy!

INDEX

Photo by Corey Sandler

ABOUT THE AUTHOR

DIANA KEUILIAN is passionate about creating wholesome versions of your favorite foods. She removes the gluten, dairy, soy, grains and cane sugar from traditional comfort food recipes like cake, tacos, cookies, waffles, enchiladas, and more. This hobby propelled her to start the popular blog RealHealthyRecipes.com, where she shares hundreds of delicious recipes and mouthwatering photos. She lives in Southern California with her husband and two young children.

For more recipes, or to contact Diana, visit RealHealthyRecipes.com and www.facebook.com/RealHealthyRecipes.